METAPUNCTUATION

Convention be damned! It's time the sacrosanct arena of commas and colons is exposed as the archaic, out-moded, illogical system it is. It's time to replace it with a new, improved, and more expressive system that fits today's communication needs. From the punctuation of fear and anxiety to dazzle rockets and boredom bombs, meta-punctuation is now, it's au courant, it's the '90s. It's also fun.

MOI

Introducing the "moi." On occasions when we wish to exult, to congratulate ourselves for a job well done, we need a sign so that the reader can gloat with us.

⇡ **"God, I'm good."**

But there can be too much of a good thing. Therefore, for pomposity (and puffballs) we have the "double moi."

⇡⇡ **"Everyone at Harvard did it."**

And for excess, for the kind of self-congratulatory statements that produce retching in the listener, we have the "triple moi."

⇡⇡⇡ **"Yes, but God, I'm good."**

And for concepts such as the "moi," heavy, filled with significance, we have the "anchor."

⇕ ?**"Do you love me, Jane."**
⇕ ?**"What is love, Bill."**

We can't answer that one. But we can bring you profundity (or is that lunacy?) in book form . . .

METAPUNCTUATION

METAPUNCTUATION

Lewis Burke Frumkes

For Alana, Timothy, and Amber

A LAUREL BOOK

Published by
Dell Publishing
a division of
Bantam Doubleday Dell Publishing Group, Inc.
1540 Broadway
New York, New York 10036

The trademark Laurel® is registered in the U.S. Patent and Trademark Office.

The trademark Dell® is registered in the U.S. Patent and Trademark Office.

ISBN: 0-440-21270-7

Printed in the United States of America

Published simultaneously in Canada

November 1993

10 9 8 7 6 5 4 3 2 1

Every text, even the most densely woven, cites them [punctuation marks] of its own accord—friendly spirits whose bodiless presence nourishes the body of language.

—THEODOR W. ADORNO

Yet I would claim that the impulse to create a second-order symbol system—a set of marks that itself refers to a set of marks—is a deep human inclination that will emerge with relatively little provocation.

HOWARD GARDNER,
The Unschooled Mind

Now here is a sentence from a popular and excellent German novel,—with a slight parenthesis in it. I will make a perfectly literal translation, and throw in the parenthesis-marks and some hyphens for the assistance of the reader,—though in the original there are no parenthesis-marks or hyphens, and the reader is left to flounder through to the remote verb the best way he can.

MARK TWAIN,
A Tramp Abroad

Contents

3

Shades, Levels, and Degrees

Spoken and written language depends to a great extent on shades, levels, and degrees. For example, there are degrees of anger in communication that can only be roughly defined without resorting to long description. With hot marks and degree signs, this anger can be clearly and succinctly stated.

4

Sexual Punctuation

Is it a male or a female speaking? I'll be darned, it's a thirtyish gentleman in a high state of lust. With the disappearance of gender terms, it's hard to know these things. Fortunately sexual metapunctuation makes everything clear. This one was described by a triple-dude sign with horns. Also, we will now be able to tell just what a prospective beau means when he says, "Hi, baby." No need to see his eyes, tongue, or body language; we will know just where he stands, and what his intentions are. Even flirt marks will be discussed.

5

The Punctuation of Fear and Anxiety

Long-overdue and much-needed marks for every type of fear, from deep panic (panic marks) to mild apprehension (fright signs). One really should be able to distinguish between a rhino bearing down on you at 60 mph, a missed period, and a full-blown hyperspastic, hyperventilating anxiety attack. Fright signs,

panic marks, and yeeks dominate this chapter.
Not for the faint of heart.

6   89

The Punctuation of Love and Hate

Everyone loves a lover, but we must distinguish
hysteroid dysphoria (mad heart-pounding
crush-loves), from platonic loves, from
unrequited loves. Naturally we will do it with
hearts and flower marks, etc. And what about
hate? I hate chocolate. I hate Jack. I'd like to
pull Jack's eyes out and drive spikes into his
brain. Dagger marks and venom tell us much
about peeves and dislikes.

7   115

Type Emphasis and Converted Musical Notation

Specific meanings for the various type sizes.
Read #24, for example, to mean stentorian, #9
as whisper.
          Adapting musical notation to the
reading of text. Most text has rhythm and
cadences that should be announced to the
reader through appropriate musical
representations.

8   139

Dazzle Rockets and Boredom Bombs

Self-explanatory. There are passages, ideas,
bursts of creativity that simply deserve dazzle
rockets, while certain other passages are
weighed down by their own tedium.

INTRODUCTION

Let's face it, American English can be very confusing. Sometimes we can clear up the confusion by just explaining ourselves further, as I am doing now, but other times the difficulty resides in the language itself. Let me illustrate:

"I love you" can have any of a hundred meanings. "I love you" can refer to sexual love, platonic love, fatherly love, or romantic love, or it can be just an expression of admiration, adoration, or gratitude, right? "I love you" can refer to a male talking to a female, a female talking to a female, a male talking to a male, a little girl talking to a flower, or even a bulldog talking to a miniature schnauzer. So when the object of your affection says, "I love you," which of the hundred meanings does he/she mean?

English, you see, is full of nuances and subtleties that give it wonderful character and range but also add to its ambiguity. Most of its richness comes from its enormous vocabulary, upward of a million words, which permits for both precise and colorful expression and which has been growing larger for centuries. Unfortunately, however, for all its complexity and breadth, the English language makes use of only a handful or so of basic symbols, devices, and marks to help with communication, to indicate rests, moods, intentions, pauses, pitch, and stresses. Despite their obvious importance, these marks of punctuation, namely the familiar period, comma, colon, question mark, exclamation point, and quotation mark, have not multiplied the same way vocabulary has. And to make matters worse, when punctuation marks are used, they are often used poorly and in obfuscating ways. Why, for heaven's sake, should a question mark appear at the end of a sentence in English, when it makes far better sense to put it at the beginning as certain other languages do? With the question mark at the beginning, the reader has time to prepare his interrogative inflection.

To my way of thinking, our few guiding symbols are both overworked and underequipped for the complicated job at hand, that of regulating texts and clarifying our language. Why not augment the existing punctuation with a new, fully hybrid notational system to take account of the myriad inflections and tones in our language? Why not have symbols that can tell us what the speaker means when he says, "I love you"? Indeed, why not develop new punctuation more in keeping with today's usage?

To this end, I have created metapunctuation.

With metapunctuation, "I love you" will no longer be a problem. You'll know if he loves you deeply enough to climb the highest mountain for you, or swim the mightiest ocean. No uncertainty here. There will be symbols such as the "delta sarc" to indicate spoken sarcasm and the "sigh" to emphasize resignation. ?Was Rock being sarcastic when he suggested I go fishing. With a delta sarc you would know. ?Now do you get the idea. ?And tell the truth, don't you prefer the question mark at the beginning.

In *Metapunctuation*, I will explain the differences between the "antipause" and the "babble," the "stream-of-consciousness mark" and the "crescendo." God knows there are hundreds, if not thousands, of emotions and shadings present in our everyday discourse that need clarification. ?Why should a reader have to figure them out like a puzzle.

Metapunctuation will make our language many times more efficient by simply adding intonational cues and other useful indicators and signifiers. Without doubt it will increase our ability to communicate with one another and understand one another. No more stupid fights with Susan when you were really talking about the same thing. ?What could be more important.

?And finally, am I serious about metapunctuation and its potential impact on American English, or do I have my tongue firmly esconced in my cheek. With the proper notation, you would know.

1

BEGINNING AND END PUNCTUATION

The workhorse and principal structural unit of written English, as you probably know, is the single sentence. Stitched together, and organized intelligently, single sentences in sequence become the foundation for good prose, poetry, and everyday discourse. When sentences run together, however, slipshod and unbroken, as they do after you have had too much coffee, or in freshman compositions, the result is often a meaningless hodgepodge and difficult to read. "Believe it or not what you will be in your next incarnation is determined almost entirely by the last two digits of your birth year thus if you happen to be born in 1945 you will be reincarnated as a fly yes a fly yes I'm sorry I know you would rather have come back as a jewel or a Rolls-Royce but you are quite unmistakably a fly . . ." You get the idea.

So grammarians have devised punctuation, i.e., standardized marks, to divide the sentences into discrete events, to orchestrate the pauses and stops, the pitch and stresses, and to make the sentences easy for us to read.

The period, for example, tells us that a sentence has come to an end. You should wait before beginning a new sentence.

The question mark tells us that the sentence is actually a question, and also that it is over.

The exclamation point tells us that a particular sentence should be emphasized.

This is fine for the period, which stops us where it should. It is not fine as far as I am concerned for the question mark or the exclamation point, nor for a number of other new signs that will debut here.

These signs should come at the beginning of the sentence, where they can tell us more about the author's intention. At present the capital letter is the only punctuation mark we use in front to signal that a new sentence is beginning. Notice, this sentence begins with a capital N.

All we have in the way of beginning and end punctuation, then, to separate and modify millions of words and an almost infinite number of combinational sentences are the period, question mark, exclamation point, and a capital letter. And the capital letter is the only one that comes at the beginning of the sentence. Clearly we need more. Enter metapunctuation.

Metapunctuation, at least much of it, comes at the beginning of the sentence in the same way that you say to someone, "May I ask you a question?" You don't first ask the question and then say, "I just asked you a question." In written English, punctuation that indicates tone or intention should come first, and with metapunctuation it does. It also tells you a great deal more in terms of what the author is trying to convey than just when to rest or stop.

⚠ THE DELTA SARC

The delta sarc indicates spoken sarcasm:

⚠ "I'll just bet you do."

⚠ ? "Brilliant, Daryl, now what do we do."

Suppose, for example, the sentence is very long, such as: "The war in Iraq was a splendid example of the kind of job we Americans can do when we put our minds to it and roll up our sleeves—bombing the daylights out of millions of demonic Iraqi soldiers trained to pull out our eyes and eat our children—wouldn't you say?" You cannot inflect the sentence until you come to the very end and discover it is a question. This makes for hasty, abrupt, and awkward changes in your reading.

In the case above, the author was also being sarcastic. A delta sarc should have appeared alongside the question mark at the beginning of the sentence to signal the reader that the author was asking a sarcastic question. ?Why should the reader remain ignorant of the author's intentions until he has already read the sentence and then have to quickly change or add the proper inflection. Nor should the reader have to wait for the adverbial modifiers, "he said sarcastically," "she said sarcastically," for example, dangling clumsily at the end to clue him in. The reader should be properly notified early on as to the author's intentions, thereby alleviating the need for many boring and repetitive adverbial modifiers—he said, she said, they barked angrily, he allowed, she screamed—and allowing him to read the sentence properly from the outset. Thus the Iraq sentence should have read:

⚠?The war in Iraq was a splendid example of the kind of job we Americans can do when we put our minds to it and roll up our sleeves—bombing the daylights out of millions of demonic Iraqi soldiers trained to pull out our eyes and eat our children—wouldn't you say.

Now it is possible that grammatical purists will accuse me of introducing my own notation and calling it punctuation. And they would be correct. However, what is punctuation if not a series of conventions or notations invented to assist in clarifying the rhythms and meanings of written language in order to help us communicate. Whatever notation serves this purpose efficiently seems worthwhile to me. The punctuation we currently use has served us well for thousands of years, but today's expanded usage requires a more powerful instrumentation. The old punctuation desperately needs revitalizing and recruiting. Language, including punctuation, is a dynamic living organism that requires proper maintenance and growth to remain healthy. Metapunctuation is designed to meet the linguistic and communication needs not only of today, but also of tomorrow. And while I've got you, I should also point out that, with the exception of those marks that stipulate they are to be used only in certain places, i.e., only at the beginning or only at the end, the choice with the others is up to you. You may sigh here or sigh there—if you prefer. As for quotation marks and metapunctuation, you may place your metapunctuation either inside or outside the quotation marks. I have done both throughout the book to show you how it looks both ways. What follows is beginning and end metapunctuation:

⊙   **THE HALT**

While a period correctly comes at the end of a sentence and signals the end of a complete statement, the halt, which also comes at the end, stops the statement with finality. It is stronger, darker, and larger than the period, more abrupt. It says to the reader this is a serious stop—do not dare move beyond until the air has cleared. The halt is often found at the end of statements that have their own apodictic logic and bear no refutation.

"God is nigh" ⊙

A halt is appropriate after this statement, which comes at the end of taps, regardless of whether or not you know what "nigh" means. Okay, it means "near." I'll bet you've been wondering what "nigh" means ever since you were at summer camp, or in the army—?right. ?Aren't you glad you bought this book. ?And don't you think a question mark is clearer at the beginning of a question rather than the end.

"That's all, folks" ⊙

This statement, usually uttered by Porky Pig at the end of Looney Tunes and Merrie Melodies cartoons, tells you the cartoon is over, finis, kaput. It deserves a halt.

"From now on anyone who speaks is a 'doofus'" ⊙

Since no one wants to be a "doofus," no one will speak. A halt is appropriate here.

"Platooooooon, halt" ⊙

"Ready, aim, fire" ⊙

"I'm afraid, Margaret, that it's the end of the line" ⊙

"That's it, I quit" ⊙

♪ THE CRESCENDO

The crescendo indicates that the sentence is going to build, like anger, or like an orgasm. It has been missing from written English for too long. It has many important uses and must of necessity come at the beginning of the sentence. The reader needs time, after all, to follow the crescendo. Some examples of crescendoing sentences are:

♪ "If I have to tell you one more time, Sitz-fleisch, I'll explode."

♪ "Heeeeerrre's Johnnnny." (Substitute whomever you'd like for Johnny. And do your best Ed McMahon imitation.)

♪ "Let's hear it for Bobby."

♪ "It's coming closer, and closer, and closer."

♪ "Hooray, hooray, hooooray."

♆ THE REVERSE CRESCENDO

The reverse crescendo is used when things wind down or become softer, gentler, quieter. As a train grinds to a stop, or when anger slowly dissipates.

♆ "Whoaaa."

♆ "I hate you, you sonofabitch, I hate you, I hate you . . . I love you, I love you, I love you."

♆ "There she goes, Miss America."

ᗡᗡᗡ "It's coming toward us, closer, closer, it's overhead now, there it goes, zzzzzooowww-mmmm."

⸮ THE SIGH

The sigh is used to emphasize resignation, as when there is literally nothing more one can do.

⸮"Oh, well. I guess so."

Or the resigned sigh of distant admiration:

⸮?"Isn't she magnificent."

⸮"Okay, okay."

⸮*"Les jeux sont fait."*

⸮"All right, you caught me."

⸮"God, I hope so."

∨ THE AWE

The awe is closely related to the sigh, except for one subtle difference. Instead of acceptance or passivity, it expresses an active and hopeful admiration as in:

∨?"Isn't she magnificent."

∨"Wow, I've never seen one like that."

∨"Now, that's a steak."

∨"You are the best."

∨"My God, look at that."

∨"That is the most delicious thing I've ever tasted."

∨?"You speak thirty-seven languages."

⊂ THE ENVY

The envy expresses envy that is often not betrayed by the words themselves.

⊂"I like that dress you're wearing."

⊂"He has a magnificent home in Cambridge."

It can be more obvious, but then it just reinforces the words.

⊂"He made $40,000,000 in the market last year."

⊂?"Not that I would trade places, but have you seen his incredible new yacht, *The Penis*."

♦ THE DISGUST

Sometimes you wish to show your disapproval without actually spelling it out. Use the disgust mark. Use it at the beginning or end, whenever you feel disgusted.

♦?"Do you believe what he named his yacht."

♦"Feel free, if you wish."

♦"He's got six mistresses." (Not to be confused with the envy.)

♦"I don't really like spiders."

♦?"Grape-Nuts and sauerkraut."

♦"The idea of beating puppies is not something I subscribe to."

♦♦ THE DOUBLE DISGUST

The double disgust registers outright repugnance.

♦♦?"Do you believe what he named his yacht."

"He just ordered roach sushi"♦♦

"Please don't eructate again at this dinner table, Garfoil. ?Do I make myself clear"♦♦

♦♦♦ THE TRIPLE DISGUST

This is a rare symbol, seldom seen and reserved for the ugliest situations or reactions.

?"Do you believe what he named his yacht"♦♦♦

"Charlotte, he just puked out of his ears"♦♦♦

?"Electrocuting him six times to make sure he's dead is really overdoing it, don't you think"♦♦♦

○ THE RING OF INDIGNATION

The ring of indignation clearly intoned from the inception of a sentence tells the reader or listener that the author is indignant about something said or something that occurred just prior to the sentence. Perhaps the author has been mistaken for someone twice his age, or called short on brains. These are genuine reasons for indignation. The ring of indignation conveys these feelings; exclamation points or question marks here are just not enough.

○"I beg your pardon, Mr. President."

○?"You think I'm fifty years old. ?Do you have astigmatism"○

Use the ring of indignation at the beginning or end.

?"You thought my novel sucked, did you"○

"No, it's not Spam, it's the finest baked Virginia ham, for your information"○

"Yes, I think I'm capable of deciding that for myself"○

⊗ TRIPLE-RINGED INDIGNATION

Triple-ringed indignation is reserved for serious offenses. Often mistaken for a Ballantine sign or a Venn diagram, it marks the most serious cause of breakup between friends. It says, not only do you insult me, but you embarrass me to no end. I want nothing more to do with you.

⊗"I do not now, nor did I ever, wear ballet slippers to bed, Rocky. I don't know where you get such notions. I have been nose guard on this team for ten years, mostly protecting your ass, and I resent the implication. ?Would you care for me to rearrange your face."

⊗?"My breath smells like what."

?"Say what"⊗

☻ THE ASTRACAN

The astracan is used to express astonishment, as when a star falls through the roof into someone's home and he says:

☻?"Am I seeing things, Mary, or is that a star."

Occasionally an ordinary person cannot believe a celebrity is saying hello to him and utters absurd remarks in astonishment. These remarks need to be acknowledged for what they are.

"Uh, uh, uh, wh, wh, wh, uh, I, I—" ☻

☻"Th-th-thank you, Your Highness, I mean, Mr. President."

?"John MacEnroe, eh. Say something obscene and prove it" ☻

Sometimes one exceeds his own expectation in something. As in:

☻"Wow, I can't believe I hit it over the fence."

"Sorry, Mr. Tyson, I didn't mean to hit you that hard" ☻

?"Did you say I got an 800 in math" ☻

◉ THE STARTLE

The startle resembles the astracan but suggests momentary fright or panic, where the astracan does not. For example:

◉"Oh! It's only you, the butler. For a moment I thought it was the mad strangler."

◉?"Who's there. I heard you move. Show yourself, damn it!"

◉"Whoaa. You gave me a moment there, young fella."

▬ THE RESPECT BAR

The respect bar is used when meeting someone of great accomplishment or age.

▬"General Schwartzkopf, what a great pleasure to have you drop in like this."

?"How old did you say you were—114. That's terrific, sir" ▬

▬"I've always admired people who could run the mile in ten seconds, especially when a giant squid is chasing them."

Or it can be used with an inanimate object in certain cases.

■■ "I love touching all this fresh currency. The mint is a wonderful place."

■■ "A fifteen-carat gem emerald, right here in the palm of my hand."

◖ THE ARCH SANC

The arch sanc conveys dripping sanctimony. It is an irritating, self-important, full-o'-oneself message. Sometimes we see it in older, seemingly wiser persons toward younger, less experienced people. But if the speaker were really wise, he probably wouldn't express sanctimony. Sanctimony actually tells us this person is narrow-minded and bigoted, someone who must build himself up at someone else's expense. Thus people who consider themselves better than other people tend to be sanctimonious. People who are clubby and cliquey are sanctimonious. Sanctimony is not the kind of thing you want to express, but if you have to, we should at least have a mark for it: the arch sanc.

"I'm sorry, my dear, but blondes are really not the kind of people we encourage to join this club" ◖

◖"Listen, Rock, not that we don't appreciate you, but you kind of smell— ?You know what I mean. !You smell, Rock."

"Daryl, baby, you're putting on a little weight, you know"◗

"Blue is the color we wear, dear"◗

◗ "I'm afraid you don't really fit in— ?Mr. 'Daryl,' is it."

?"You do have a yacht, don't you"◗

◗?"You call him tough, man. Daryl couldn't kiss my freon."

◗?"Tenure. I'm afraid that's not even a consideration in your case."

◗"Bald people, you know, bear to be watched."

◗?"Harvard? ?Did you say H-H-Harvard, Rock. Think rather Honolulu State, my boy."

As you can see, there is unfortunately no limit to the forms sanctimony can take. While it should earn a double disgust, I'm afraid the best we can do in all fairness is mark it with a ◗.

⌃   THE ANSWER MARK

The natural counterpart of the question mark, which correctly belongs at the beginning of a sentence, the answer mark correctly belongs at the end of the sentence—to tell you the question has been answered. Sometimes it is hard to know whether a question has been answered. In fact, some questions are answered by another question. In such a case, the question mark at the beginning of the sentence should be followed by an answer mark to tell you that the question you asked in the first place has been answered by the second question. *Capice*?

"Thirty-three" ∧

"Paris" ∧

"Only when he does it to you first" ∧

"When I feel like it" ∧

Or, as in the case mentioned above, when the question is answered by another question, as for example in rhetorical questions.

?"Does a bee buzz" ∧

?"What do you think" ∧

?"Do bears live in the woods" ∧

?"Are you for real" ∧

?And now that we've reached the end of the chapter, what could be more fitting than the fin. ∧

● **THE FIN**

The fin means the end—that's it. !It's over,
baby ●

Symbol Summary

BEGINNING AND END PUNCTUATION

△ THE DELTA SARC—Indicates spoken sarcasm.

⊙ THE HALT—Signals the end of a complete statement. Stronger than a period.

𝒮 THE CRESCENDO—Indicates that a sentence is going to build.

℺ THE REVERSE CRESCENDO—Things wind down, become softer.

𝒮 THE SIGH—Emphasizes resignation.

∨ THE AWE—Expresses hopeful admiration.

⊂ THE ENVY—Expresses envy not betrayed by words themselves.

● THE DISGUST—Shows implicit disapproval.

●● **THE DOUBLE DISGUST**—Registers repugnance.

●●● **THE TRIPLE DISGUST**—Total disgust, repugnance.

○ **THE RING OF INDIGNATION**—Conveys indignation.

⊗ **TRIPLE-RINGED INDIGNATION**—Reserved for serious offenses.

◓ **THE ASTRACAN**—Expresses astonishment.

◔ **THE STARTLE**—Suggests momentary fright or panic.

■ **THE RESPECT BAR**—Used in the presence of someone of great accomplishment or age.

◖ **THE ARCH SANC**—Conveys dripping sanctimony.

∧ **THE ANSWER MARK**—The natural counterpart of the question mark.

● **THE FIN**—That's it.

INTRODUCTION TO EXERCISES

To get you into the swing of things, I have provided answers for the first set of exercises, but only the first set. I have introduced two characters, Daryl and Rock, to try to express the range of beginning and end punctuation. Curiously, you will notice that Rock and Daryl do not use every metapunctuational symbol from the chapter. This is because Daryl and Rock are stupid and cannot remember all the marks. Had I used Percy and Marge, all the marks from the chapter would have appeared. On the other hand, by using Daryl and Rock, I am actually trying to make a point. Not every symbol, you see, is necessary or relevant to this particular exercise, and we should use metapunctuation only when and where it is appropriate. Metapunctuation is best when it is natural, not contrived. So Rock and Daryl will work here after all.

As you finish each chapter, I urge you to do the exercises that follow it until you are comfortable using the full metapunctuation notation system. Eventually you will do it automatically. Thus, for the next chapter, "Interior Punctuation," you should not only use whatever notation you have learned in the new chapter, but also employ any beginning and end metapunctuation. Learning is cumulative.

Good luck!

EXERCISES

⊂∨"Rock, I love that new leather jacket you bought the other day. The one with the spikes and chains."

⋔♦?"Do you, Daryl. ?How come you didn't say you liked it when I was buying it."

■"Because Pancake said it was dorky. That's why."

⌘♦". . . C'mon, Daryl. ?Because Pancake didn't like it, you didn't like it."

○ ■"Look, Rock. You know I think you have the best taste in clothes. It's just that, well, I think Pancake has good taste too."

♦♦"Daryl, you are a jerk."

☯○?"Why am I a jerk, Rock. ?Because I think your girlfriend has good taste too∧ ?What's jerky about that. ?She picked you, didn't she."

𝄞♦♦♦"Get lost, Daryl. You are a fool, and a jerk, and an idiot."

○☺∨"I can't believe you're saying that, Rock. You're my best friend."

♦♦♦⊗"Yeah, you're my best friend too, Daryl. But you're a lowlife, weasily chicken liver. ?Because you couldn't stand up to Pancake, you had to side with her. And then today you tell me you really like the jacket. ?How disgusting can you get."

૧■∨"Okay, okay, I'm a lowlife, Rock. But I still think you're the greatest."

☺!"Uh oh."

?"What."

"Nothing ∧ I thought that was Pancake walking in."

ℬ?"Daryl, let's drop this discussion, okay. Like finis, no more. ?*Capice*."

"But Rock . . ."

"I said, that's it"●

2

INTERIOR
PUNCTUATION

Okay, beginning and end punctuation are important, but what about the inside? I'm glad you asked. While beginning and end punctuation set the tone and parameters of written discourse, it is the interior punctuation that gives it character and rhythm. Here I have in mind antipauses, babbles, and diddledy dots, among other marks. What are we to do, for example, when we encounter a Woolf-ian passage of almost incomprehensible cadences? Or your own—ahem, ahem—shall we say rather dense and unusual prose? Why, we use a stream-of-consciousness mark, of course, to suggest pure unadulterated flow.

∿THE BABBLE

Not only gossips babble. Sometimes people who are hyped from too much coffee or enthusiasm babble. People who have been alone too long bab-ble. They mean well but they babble. They babble and there is no way to shut them off. It has to do with the velocity of their words and the number per square inch. They remind you of thirty-three RPM records being played at seventy-eight.

∿"So John took out Marsha and they went to the movies and then he bought her popcorn, and you know, they sat through the movie, and when it was over he took her for a drive. ?Can you imagine.

I am just so fascinated. ?Did I tell you about Sheila. Well, Sheila . . ."

⌒⌒⌒?"Whaddya wanna do, John. ?How about the movies. ?How about bowling. ?How about drinking it up with the guys at Mario's. ?How about hanging out on Third Street. ?Whaddya think, John, the movies, hanging out, drinking it up with the guys. ?Maybe the movies, right, John. ?Or drinking it up, or bowling, right, John. ?Or . . ."

– – –THE STREAM-OF-CONSCIOUSNESS MARK

As contrasted with the babble, the stream-of-consciousness mark just flows, and flows, and flows, wherever it goes, whatever thoughts or ideas occur, whatever images present themselves, just on and on. Thus:

– – –Maybe I will or maybe I won't. !Gosh, she was pretty— ?I wonder when next I'll see her, you like music, don't you. Of course you do—red green a window—there is hardly any connection between the thoughts or logic contained therein. Abadab-adbbaababdaadda doooooo.

Or:

– – –"Whoa, I'm imagining an iron horse with a horn, it's a unicorn, only virgins can see unicorns, maybe I'm a virgin, maybe I'm an extravirgin like olive oil, that's ridiculous, I'm not an extravirgin, that's odd, then ?why am I seeing a unicorn, ?and why an iron unicorn, maybe I'm seeing a unihorn, which is different perhaps from a unicorn, a ferrous unihorn, that's what I'm seeing, whoa, I'm glad I solved that. ?But what's this. The Lone Ranger on a unihorn, whoa, that's heavy, maybe there were too many raisins in my cereal this morning. ?What am I thinking. ?Why am I thinking, whoa. . . ."

⃝ THE ANTIPAUSE

The antipause indicates that one should move along, not stop. Unlike a comma, or period, or halt, it wants you to keep going. Go on, it says, go on, move along.

⃝"Don't stop here after just one orgasm."

⃝"Notice there are no stops."

⃝"That's what I think, but perhaps not . . . or perhaps."

⃝!"Okay. ?But do you think . . ."

∴ THE DIDDLEDY DOT

The diddledy dot is used to indicate frivolity.

∴?"Oh ho, he makes $4,000,000 a year, does he."

⁙?"Sorry, did I get that mayonnaise in your hair."

⁙?"No kidding, you like chicken rumps too."

⁙?"You are going to paint your house what color."

⁙"La da dee da da da daaa."

〈 THE SIGH

The sigh, introduced in Chapter 1 to indicate resignation, can come at any point within a statement or at the beginning or end. The sigh may also be used to indicate admiration or appreciation. Let us review the sigh of resignation:

〈"At last, this is the last mile."

〈"Well, I guess that's it."

〈?"What else can we do."

〈?"Checkmate, eh."

〈?"What am I going to do with you, Harold."

Now the sigh of admiration or appreciation:

〈?"Isn't she magnificent."

𝄈?"Will you look at that."

𝄈"Thank God."

𝄈?"Can you believe that."

𝄈"Those is what I call legs."

𝄈"The view from this balloon of the Sonoran Desert is absolutely breathtaking."

𝄈"I've never seen anything that chocolaty."

As an afternote, perhaps it should be mentioned that the sigh of admiration that is sometimes expressed by the word "oh" is often followed by the word "wow," while the sigh of resignation accompanied by the word "oh" is usually followed by "dear." Naturally, these words need not appear at all.

✎ THE GIBBER

The gibber is a relatively rare sign that indicates gibberish is being spoken here. Usually an author does not refer to his own work as gibberish, but may instead be quoting some pseudoauthorial reference that he feels is gibberish or a literary work that he does not admire.

✎ And in the immortal words of Rhabindanrath Amin, "Golly gook, awesome rathbone, at will."

⊘ God is the infinite erupting into the finite.

☾ **THE FEY**

Sometimes a text is one of mystical enchantment or otherworldliness or magic, and you want to convey that impression beyond the literality of the words. Metapunctuation provides the fey.

☾ Into the woods she disappeared, and then almost at once and yet a million years from now, she reappeared in a bower of stars. . . .

☾ There was something afoot, but Dunwood was not sure what.

☾ The creature appeared to be staring at us, yet its eyes were closed. . . .

☾ The secret fragrance of this tea is the oil of bergamot, a pear-shaped citrus found in the Mediterranean.

☺ **THE GLEE**

Now we are in the realm of laughter and delight—a mood of merriment setting the tone. It is important to convey this mood with glees. Glees are like salt or pepper and may be sprinkled wherever you feel the need.

☻ "Omigod, I won the lottery."

☻ "One more time, please, pretty please, just one more time."

☻ And then, just as the announcer walked to the microphone, she began to sense the victory at hand.

☻ "Now let's try the dragon coaster, then the octopus."

☻ !"Then cotton candy."

◊ **THE TRISTE**

There are occasions, sometimes without warning, when sadness is the order of the day, when tears well up in the eyes and voices become tremulous. It is appropriate in such situations to use the triste.

◊ As the little girl's turtle started across the street, an oncoming car, unaware of the small, plodding creature in front of it . . .

◊ "He was a remarkable person, someone who truly cared."

◊ ?"Will I never see you again, Rebecca."

◊ "I'm sorry, Lawrence."

ᵟᵇ"I'm glad that you two were friends, and that you both had the opportunity to glitter together awhile in the literary skies." (John Wallace)

˅ˊ   THE GRRR

We all get angry. Don't pretend you don't. We seethe, we boil, we rage. The grrr is an anger sign that can be enhanced in several ways. One way is with degree marks (see Chapter 3); the other is by increasing the number of *r*'s in the grrr. Since we all may envision endless *r*'s in a rage, the max should be five. This can be augmented with degree marks if necessary. Let's begin with mild anger:

˅ˊ "I told you not to do that, Rock."

˅ˊ "Don't give me the finger, Daryl."

˅ˊ "I'll give you the finger when you deserve it, Rock."

Now seething:

˅ˊˊ "Daryl, give me the finger once more and I'll rearrange your nose."

˅ˊˊ "Don't even dream about it, Rock."

Let's boil:

˅ˊˊˊ "That's it, Daryl, that's it."

\"""!"Get away from me, Rock."

Rage:

\""""!"I'm gonna kill you."

\""""!"Not if I kill you first, you @#@%&*."

↥   **THE MOI**

There are times, occasions, when we all wish to exult, to congratulate ourselves for a job well done, for an accomplishment or triumph. At such times we need a sign of exultation so the reader may exult with us. The moi is such a sign.

↥"I can't believe I did it."

↥"!Ahhh. At last."

↥"There it is. The finished manuscript: *Meta-punctuation*."

↥"Ginger, you are mine at last."

↥"There in the mirror I see genius."

↥"It's been a long time coming."

↥"God, I'm good."

↥"Congratulations, Jack."

↑"Thanks."

↑"I'd say it's a pretty fair job."

↑"Not too bad."

↑"It's ours."

↑?"Remember the Hope Diamond. *!Voilà.*"

〰〰   **THE DOUBLE MOI**

While the moi signifies self-congratulation in a deserved way, the double moi means that the individual has become filled with pomposity beyond any measure of his accomplishment and is now gloating in an obnoxious way.

〰〰"You are mine now, Carol, all mine, heh, heh."

〰〰"Yes, it was a mild feat of genius, but not as difficult as you might imagine."

〰〰"Now I've got it, and fuck the rest of the world."

〰〰"Here it is, !but wait. Don't get too near. That's it, stay over there."

ꝳꝳ "The world has waited a long time for this. And now I, Emmous K. Gilderschmidt, have provided it."

ꝳꝳꝳ THE TRIPLE MOI

The triple moi means that this person's sense of grandeur is such that you want to throw up.

ꝳꝳꝳ "I, Matt McCall, am an artiste."

ꝳꝳꝳ ?"Carol is mine, so why don't you just stick it."

ꝳꝳꝳ "It was nothing."

ꝳꝳꝳ !"God, I'm good."

Ӿ A WORD ABOUT PAUSALS

Pausals are used in place of knowledge to fill the gaps and ellipses in our speech. Because of the frequency with which they lace our discourses, they require symbols.

Ӿ This is the symbol for "you know," by far the most popular of the current crop of pausals.

I'd like to go Ӿ, but I can't. Ӿ how it is, Ӿ, if I could, I would, Ӿ.

⌐This is the symbol for "uh," somewhat old-fashioned but still very much with us.

Ladies and gentlemen, I'd, ∟, like to tell you a, ∟, few things about, ∟, the company.

⋈ This is the symbol for "agh," the least of the pausal weeds but the choice of some.

⚓ THE ANCHOR

The anchor suggests that the subject under discussion is heavy, profound, deep. Perhaps you are trying to understand the significance of cold dark matter in space, or the meaning of the Boötes void. These astronomical concepts have cosmological ramifications that deserve to be read slowly and appreciated, not glossed over lightly. They deserve an anchor mark.

⚓?"But suppose that the underlying cosmological structure of the larger universe turns out to be part of one giant cosmic organism. ?Is that organism God."

⚓?"Do you believe that life on earth is the result of directed panspermia, that we are all self-replicating bio-automata, created by higher intelligences from another world."

⚓?"Do you love me, Jane."

↕?"What is love, Bill."

↕?"What do you think about the idea of metapunctuation as a new metalanguage."

↕!Anchors away.

SYMBOL SUMMARY

INTERIOR PUNCTUATION

〰️ **THE BABBLE**—The babble indicates the speaker is unable to control the flow of speech.

– – – **THE STREAM-OF-CONSCIOUSNESS MARK**—Flows and flows and flows.

↻ **THE ANTIPAUSE**—Move along, don't stop.

✺ **THE DIDDLEDY DOT**—Indicates frivolity.

♉ **THE SIGH**—Indicates resignation or admiration.

⊚ **THE GIBBER**—Indicates gibberish is being spoken.

☪ **THE FEY**—Mysticism and otherworldliness afoot.

☺ THE GLEE—Indicates merriment.

♂ THE TRISTE—Indicates sadness.

✓ THE GRRR—Indicates anger.

↑ THE MOI—Exultation.

↑↑ THE DOUBLE MOI—Extreme self-congratulation.

↑↑↑ THE TRIPLE MOI—Megalomania.

⤲ YOU KNOW—The most popular pausal.

∪ UH—Old standby pausal.

⋈ AGH—A less used pausal.

⇕ THE ANCHOR—Heavy discussion under way.

EXERCISES

Try your hand at inserting metapunctuation where appropriate in the following exercise.

FRUMKES'S RULES FOR TRAVELING

Everyone needs to travel, if not for the sheer exhilaration and sense of adventure that attends boarding an airplane for exotic climes, then just to pile up frequent flyer miles. So let's talk travel.

To really enjoy traveling, you must have a good time while away, and you must avoid any unpleasant experiences on returning, such as not being able to find your baggage at the terminal. The baggage problem grows especially vexing after a seventeen-hour flight from Florida during which time the pilot tries unsuccessfully to locate his contact lens in his soup and flies by mistake to Toledo. You are in kill mode, nerves shot, eyes small and beady. At moments such as these, exiting the plane at La Guardia with even two or three tons of hand luggage to carry can be exhausting. Your mood is not improving. You follow the other passengers through millions of miles of corridors, which finally let you out at a baggage claim somewhere in Idaho where no limousine driver is waiting for you with a big sign reading FRUMPKINS. However, a herd of mangy, angry people are jockeying for position around a conveyor belt. Football tackles and Mafia chieftains are in the front row.

"That's it, Rock, grab it!"

"You grab it, Daryl!"

"#**&!!#, dang, damn, I missed."

"Grab it, Daryl! Grab it!"

"I got it, Rock, uh oh! My back, my back, Rock, my back is out, help, help!"

"Don't worry, Daryl, I've got the bag with the oranges."

Had Daryl and Rock consulted Frumkes's rules for easy baggage recovery at the airport, Daryl would simply have yelled, "Rock, I dropped the tarantulas," then picked up the luggage and left as the other tourists scattered. And you can do the same. Substitute "spiders," "ticks," "bees," or "nerve gas" for tarantulas if you prefer. They all work. This is the kind of practical advice you won't find in standard travel books.

Is that right, Lewis? What are some of the other rules?

TIP LIBERALLY—Essentially this means tip big. I ask you the following conundrum: Under equally rainy conditions, who do you think will get the taxi—Rock, dressed in torn jeans and a Mohawk haircut, holding a sign that reads "I don't tip," or Daryl, in the Brooks Brothers suit, who is smiling and waving a fifty-dollar bill? The answer, of course, is Daryl. Cabbies are not stupid, you know. They want summer homes in the Hamptons too. In order to test the magic of big tipping, leave a hundred-dollar tip for the waiter next time you have a cup of coffee. If I am correct, the waiter will make his gratitude known to you in subtle ways such as licking you or saying, "May I kiss your shoes, sir?"

LEAVE PETS AT HOME—Especially serpents and rodents. For some ungodly reason, other travelers don't enjoy it when your child introduces them to his pet garter snake or rat at the pool. These unsophisticated sunbathers (of whom there are many) have a tendency to scream "Help!" at the top of their lungs and climb to the tippy top of their chaise longue. Why cause a commotion? Police are not fun to deal with. It's just easier to leave the pet home. Even your pet Doberman, "Throat-ripper," sweet as he is, may cause apprehension in other guests if he stares at them as if they were hamburgers and utters a low growl. Leave him home with a few carcasses until you return. Stuffed animals, however, are not considered pets. You may take as many stuffed animals with you as you wish.

GO ONLY TO THE BEST PLACES—As with most things in life, aim for the best. The Breakers, the Boca Raton Hotel & Club, and Fisher Island in Florida, the White Elephant in Nantucket, the Ritz Carlton in Boston, the Arizona Biltmore in Phoenix, and the Carlisle in New York. These are places that will make your vacation special just by virtue of being the best. You will meet the best people, eat the best food, play the best golf and tennis, have the best accommodations. Odalisques will dance for you by night and giant eunuchs will fan you by day. Attendants will anoint your body with fragrant oils. The best instructors will instruct you. In other words, you will have the best time. And you can afford these places too, because they cost only eighteen billion trillion dollars a day. Oh? You're not the Sultan of Brunei? Not even Donald Trump? You're the coat check at Wendy's. So sorry. Anyway, I know you love Lulu's Bella Vista in Asbury Park where you've been staying for the last thirty-five years, and that you have a Lulu's T-shirt and know Lulu's theme song. Good news! Lulu's got a room waiting for you and it's your old favorite, No. 324, on the third level over the parking lot. Go for it!

BE PREPARED—Always take a bottle opener with you. You never know when you will need it to open a bottle of ginger ale. In the absence of modern technology, opening a ginger ale in Fiji may prove a real challenge. You might try jumping on it. Nope, jumping up and down on it does nothing but hurt your foot. Twisting the top with a palm frond will rip the frond. Trying to push the cap up with your finger, even if you are very strong, just leaves red dents in your finger. More than likely you will grow frustrated at this point and throw the goddamn bottle through the window where it will hit someone on the head. He will report the incident to the hotel and start an action against you for $150 million. No amount of apologizing will work. The newspapers will shout CRAZED PSYCHO BEANS FAMOUS DIRECTOR WITH MISSILE. Your wife will leave you, your children will be humiliated, and your reputation will be ruined. Legal fees will wipe you out. You will become homeless, unloved, forlorn, and forgotten. God help you!

TRAVEL LIGHT—Not naked, just light. Too many bags will impede your progress when you have to make a fast getaway or catch a plane. So, what should you wear? What should you use to play tennis and golf? What should you read? What should you change into at night after bingo, you ask?

The idea here is to bring only one suitcase—full of money. Buy what you need when you arrive, then discard it when leaving. For the record, my original rule was entitled TRAVEL LIGHT, TRAVEL RICH, but I lightened it up by leaving off the second part.

SMILE—Always smile when traveling. No one likes a sourpuss. When you enter a period of turbulence on the plane and are wishing you had never left home and are making deals with the heavenly father if only he will get you to your destination safely, smile at the person sitting next to you. When you land and discover your luggage missing, especially the bag with all your jewelry and credit cards, smile as you contemplate life's little jokes. When you get to the hotel tired and in immediate need of a bath and there is no reservation in your name, smile as you summon up hitherto untapped reserves of grace and charm. When it rains every other day during your two-week vacation, smile as you realize things could be worse, and they could be. So now you're back home, and actually you're glad to be home even though the trip was fun— so smile because you're secure among familiar surroundings. And finally, smile too as you finish reading this piece with these valuable rules for traveling, and realize you don't have to make a living writing this stuff. You son-of-a-gun, don't you dare smile!

3

SHADES, LEVELS, AND DEGREES

SHADES, GHOSTS AND DEVILS

Shades, levels, and degrees are the volume and contrast controls of the language. They express intensity of emotion as well as loudness and softness. They express pitch and pith. Without them an enormous range of expression would be lost.

∧∨   SHADES

!"Take it down a shade, Rock." You bet— Rock is being boisterous, rowdy, loud. But there must be a way to indicate just when Rock has complied with our request. Just when he has lowered his voice even a small gradation. Like now.

"You see, Daryl, I can lower my voice."
But what if Rock wasn't announcing that he has lowered his voice. How would we know when he did? Yes, we could append to the sentence another modifying sentence such as:

he said, in a slightly lower voice.
But why not just indicate the lowered tone with a "down-tick." Simple and clear. One tick, one shade. Two ticks, two shades. More than two ticks and we get into levels. If Rock were taking it up a shade, we would so indicate with an up-tick. Up-ticks and down-ticks—these are how we indicate shades.

!"Mom, I wanna go home."
∧!"Mom, I wanna go home."
∧∨!"Mom, I wanna go home."

51

∧◡"For God's sake, will you lower your voice."

∧"Now this time let's hear it."

∧"Just turn up the volume a shade, will you, Daryl. . . . Thanks."

∧He glowered at her, and then, staring straight into her eyes, he said, "Never again will I be such a fool."

The up-tick is probably present in the progression of events and can be deduced, but a visual clue in the form of an up-tick is so much easier.

Another way to indicate shades is with fonts. Thus if I want to take something up a shade, I might temporarily enlarge the font size. Or conversely if I wish to take something down a shade I might reduce the font size. Ticks only go up two shades but fonts can go even higher.

So much for shades; you get the idea.

↑↓   **LEVELS**

Levels are different from shades. Levels are planes of volume on which you conduct your discourse. They move higher or lower just like shades but tend to stay there for a while. Shades are more transitory, of the moment. They also move in

smaller gradations. To know when to increase the
level of your voice if you are reading aloud, we use
an up arrow. Conversely we use a down arrow to
decrease the level.

↑"And now, ladies and gentlemen."

↓"Ladies and gentlemen, if we could just
lower our voices for a moment."

↑"This time let's sing it one level higher."

↓"I can't stand it anymore, Rock."

↓"Neither can I, Molly."

↓"You're a doofball, Rock."

↑?"Are you calling me a doofball, Molly."

"Yes I am, Rock. !Doofball, doofball,
doofball."

↑ "I can't believe that we've sunk to this level,
Molly." (In point of fact, Rock and Molly only sank
to a level figuratively. The actual volume level of
their spat increased. Thus despite the low level of
their argument, the up arrow is appropriate here.)

↑"As we approached the runway, the roar of
the jets became louder and louder."

69, 96 **DEGREES**

Degrees are terribly important. They are measures of intensity. It matters enormously, for example, whether the temperature outside is 99 or 19. It also matters enormously whether you have a first-degree burn, or a third-degree burn, or a fever of 105 or 98.7.

In language, degrees are also of great importance. If you are burning with anger, the degree of anger should register. If you are consumed with hatred, the degree to which you are consumed makes a difference. The same with love, jealousy, and most other feelings.

Degrees are superscribed like exponents above the feelings. They run from 1 to 100 just like the centigrade scale.

"^{67}I love you, Molly."
?"But how much do you love me, Rock."

With degree marks, Molly may not know, but you will. Rock loves Molly to the 67th degree. Should Molly be happy? You figure it out.

"^{87}I want that bad."
?"How bad."
"^{87}Real bad."

Just how bad you want something can also be expressed in degrees. Degrees, then, represent an option, another way of clarifying the intensity of emotions and needs. Abstract concepts such as courage and cowardice can also be illustrated with degrees.

"[93]Ready, Rock, I'm going right into the tiger's cage to save that dog."

?"[87]Did you see Daryl. He put his hand right through the bars of that tiger's cage to try to save that dog."

?"[83]Did you see Daryl. He tried to lure the tiger down to the other end of the cage, so the dog would have time to escape."

Now let's push it to the nth degree.

?"[99]Did you see Daryl. He punched the tiger right in the snout with his bare fist because it went after his dog."

?"[99]Did you see Daryl. He climbed right into the tiger's cage and kicked the tiger in the teeth. Amazing. Incredible. I will always remember Daryl."

"[78]Yeah. ?But you know what Daryl rhymes with, don't you. 'Peril.' Daryl was a big fool."

But what is a big fool? Can't we be more precise about what kind of fool Daryl was? Of course we can. Shades, levels, and degrees.

SYMBOL SUMMARY

SHADES, LEVELS, AND DEGREES

∧∨ SHADES—Shades indicate when the voice is being raised or lowered.

↑↓ LEVELS—Levels indicate the plane on which the discourse is conducted.

69, 96 DEGREES—Degrees measure the intensity of the language.

EXERCISES

?"Rock, can you hear me."
"No, Daryl, I can't hear you."
?"Now can you hear me, Rock."
"No, Daryl, I still can't hear you."
"Lunch is ready, Rock."
"I'll be there in a minute, Daryl."

?"Do you love Pancake, Rock."
"Yeah, I love Pancake, Daryl."
?"Do you love Ginger, Rock."
"Yeah, Daryl, I love Ginger too."
?"And how about Mary-Louise Puffin."
"Yeah, Goddamn it, I love her too."

?"What about you and Rapunzel, Daryl."
"I don't talk about my feelings for Rapunzel."
?"You don't talk about your feelings for Rapunzel. ?You don't talk about your feelings for Rapunzel. ?After I just told you how I felt about Pancake, and Ginger, and Mary-Louise Puffin, and you don't talk about your feelings for Rapunzel. I think I'm going to kick you for a field goal, Daryl."

4

SEXUAL
PUNCTUATION

GENDER PERFECT

The following is a letter from a University of Kentucky journalism professor to a student there. It was published in the November 1991 issue of The American Spectator.

Dear Victoria,

On your recent scholarship application, members of the review committee noticed the inappropriate use of the term "chairman." (We women of the university enjoy the support of the majority of our male colleagues in using language which is either gender inclusive or gender free when referring to a generic position.)

And, of course, it is especially inappropriate to address a woman as "chairman" unless she has specifically requested such a limiting language. (We at the School of Journalism particularly expect our News/Editorial majors to check ALL their facts; that includes making sure whether you are addressing a letter of application to a female or a male professor.)

Soon you will be entering the corporate or media sector as you begin your career. There, too, you will find there are expectations that women not be made invisible through thoughtless use of language. Attached is a pertinent example of just such thoughtless use . . . and the very public acknowledgment that it was indeed thoughtless.

If you feel your coursework has not prepared you to use gender-inclusive language in your writing, there are a number of books I would be happy to recommend. Please let me know if you wish a list.

Best regards,
S. Scott Whitlow, Ph.D.

Just the other day while taking a ride in the country, someone in our party remarked, "Wow, look at that, a woman postman," and we all laughed at the oxymoron. We also laughed because we realized the difficulty our friend was having describing what she saw, a postman, postperson, what have you, who was a female. As this book is being written, society has become increasingly aware that for too long the English language has treated women unfairly, anointing men as the dominant sex and casting women in many roles that stem from past cultural expectations and outmoded standards. Women were once supposed to be exclusively child-rearers, who stayed in the home doing motherly chores. Thus women apparently did not deliver mail as this woman did whom we passed in the car, and whom our friend had difficulty describing. In earlier periods, society was male-oriented and male-centered. Not so today.

But language has not kept up with the times and we find ourselves increasingly challenged by the need to neutralize the gender of the words we use. Cowperson rather than cowboy, salesperson rather than salesman, chair rather than chairman or chairwoman, host rather than hostess. Yet it seems to me that unless it is disparaging or simply none of our business, we want to know the gender of a person we are reading about. It helps us understand situations more clearly when we know not only whether someone is male or female, but also whether he/she is married or single, old or young, gay, bi, or straight. Sexual metapunctuation indicates clearly the information we seek, while obviating the need to struggle with a hundred variants in terminology while grammarians are sorting the problem out, and at the same time allows anonymity where called for simply by leaving the punctuation out. How simple. No more will you have to anguish over whether you should use he or she, or he/she; waiter, waitwoman, or waitperson; girl, lady, or woman. You may use whichever referent you wish or whichever is grammatically fashionable at the time—metapunctuation will convey the information you seek.

⊕⊃ HUMANMIX

No question, we need an alternative to the generic "man," which in old English meant person or human being, similar to the Latin "homo," but which evolved into a more sexist use over time. Humankind, as a word, is a good possibility, but the humanmix sign of metapunctuation is best. With the humanmix appearing in a sentence, we know exactly what we're talking about just as a gardener understands when he opens a package of seed mix. A mix of human beings, in all their wonderful variety.

⊕⊃"For all man to see."

⊕⊃"Man is an infinitely wise creature except when it comes to English grammar."

⊕⊃"Be it man or beast, or triton or titan."

① THE GENDERSPHERE

The gendersphere is the form we use to distinguish between males and females in metapunctuation, and also to denote other pertinent sexual characteristics and information. It is essentially a sphere or circle that is divided into two halves, the left representing the female and the right the male. We can shade the hemispheres, adorn them, join or separate them. In this way they function not unlike a bar code.

◖ THE LEFT HEMI-GENDERSPHERE

The female in metapunctuation is represented by a left hemi-gendersphere, just as the male is represented by a right hemi-gendersphere. Plato in the *Symposium* spoke of males and females as hemispheres seeking union, seeking to become a complete sphere. Whether or not this is the governing instinct in modern male-female relations is open to question. Nevertheless we can still represent males and females as hemispheres. With hemi-genderspheres present, we may use whatever personal pronouns and other words we wish and still be clear as to gender—which individuals are females and which males. If we see a left hemi-gendersphere unadorned, adorned, or shaded, we know the person is female.

◖"The waitperson brought the steak."

◑"The computer was manned by two experts."

◖"The speaker continued on about social correctness, political correctness, academic correctness, and sexual correctness."

◖?"Gerry, will you please pass the pizza."

◖"And now, ladies and gentlemen, may I present our esteemed first dragon, Randi Leifschleifer."

◁"The killer took careful aim through the window."

⊟ THE SHADED LEFT HEMI-GENDERSPHERE

The left hemi-gendersphere may be divided into four quadrants and shaded to display age. Thus if only the upper quadrant is shaded, the female is under twenty-five years of age. The first and second quadrants shaded would put her at between twenty-five and fifty. If the third quadrant is also shaded, she is between fifty and seventy-five. If all the quadrants are shaded, she is over seventy-five years of age. Thus:

⊟"Hello, Regina," means Regina is under twenty-five.

⊟"Hello, Regina," means Regina is between twenty-five and fifty.

⊟"Hello, Regina," means Regina is between fifty and seventy-five.

⊟"Hello, Regina," tells us that Regina is an older woman, somewhere between seventy-five and max, whatever max may be.

◁ THE UNSHADED LEFT HEMI-GENDERSPHERE

The unshaded left hemi-gendersphere means the female in question is a child or a virgin or both.

It suggests someone young and relatively inexperienced.

◁ "Here comes Amy."

◁ ?"Is it true she can see unicorns."

◁ "She looks like a tramp." Notice the words are at odds with the sign. Always trust the sign. Thus you are receiving double information.

But what if the writer does not wish to divulge information about the age of the female or her experience? Then what?

Then the author or printer simply displays a:

⊠ **THE EXED LEFT HEMI-GENDERSPHERE**

When the author does not wish to convey information about the female's age or experience or when this information is withheld for whatever reasons, an exed left hemi-gendersphere appears.

⊠ ?"Who is she."

⊠ ?"How old would you say Marlene is."

⊠ The head of the upper school rose to applause.

♂ THE RODDED LEFT HEMI-GENDERSPHERE

In metapunctuation, the way we indicate whether the female is married or unmarried is with rods affixed to the upper left curve of the hemi-gendersphere. One small rod protruding from the upper left curl of the hemi-gendersphere means the female is single or unmarried. Two rods protruding means she is married or spoken for. Three rods protruding means she is divorced or widowed. If no rods protrude, we cannot tell if she is married or unmarried. Perhaps the information is not available, or perhaps it is withheld.

♂ "Bill, I'd like you to meet Janet."

♂ "Mary Harkens, ♂ Wendy Parkens, ♂ Lily Mallory."

♂ She entered the room surrounded by a cloud of ether.

♂ ?"What did you say your name was."

♂ "Sister Katherine will escort you to your room."

♂ The owner of the boutique suddenly appeared.

ⅅ   THE RIGHT HEMI-GENDERSPHERE

The right hemi-gendersphere denotes a male. Like its left counterpart, it may be shaded to reflect age and rodded, or duded as we say with a male, once to show the male is unmarried, twice to show he is married, and three times to show he is divorced or a widower.

♭ The president took the mike and began to gyrate wildly as he spoke.

♭ A striking blond male walked into the bar and ordered a milk.

♭ Rodman sat down at his desk and picked up the plans for the atomic stomach pump his company was working on.

♭   HORNS

When the rods of the double-dude sign protruding from a right hemi-gendersphere, for example, take the form of horns, they are telling us that the gentleman in question is in a high state of sexual excitation. Horns properly belong in Chapter 6 but can be mentioned here as an alternative adornment sometimes favored by writers.

♭ "Rock, easy, baby."

ᗬ"Fine, Daryl. ?Who's that foxy-looking chick sitting at the next table."

ᗬ"That's not a foxy-looking chick, Rock. It's Bob Kovalovicz, the new auto mechanic at Frank's garage. I think you better get your eyes checked."

ᗬ"Yeah, Daryl, it was the long blond hair kinda fooled me."

ᗬᗬ WINGS

Wings, when attached to a left or right hemigendersphere, mean the individual is gay. One wing means gay, two wings means bisexual. The absence of wings simply means the individual is heterosexual. As with all metapunctuation, wings are available to use at the discretion of the writer. They are useful when certain inflections or intonations are called for, as in a play.

ᗬ"Oh, I can't stand it, it's Johnny Tambourine."

ᗬ?"Hi, Johnny, how are you."

ᗬᗬ?"And who are you, lovely creature."

ᗬᗬ"O Johnny, I'm Charles, one of your biggest fans. And this is Mike."

♭"That's wonderful, Charles. ?Would you mind getting me a drink."

♭"Of course, Johnny, your wish is my command."

SUFFIXES

In most cases, confusing suffixes such as gentle(man), post(man), milk(man), chair(man) that denote individuals of both sexes are taken care of by the use of hemi-genderspheres. Grammarians, linguists, and wordsmiths may then argue about which suffixes to use, if any, but as far as understanding is concerned, metapunctuation is all you need.

SYMBOL SUMMARY

SEXUAL PUNCTUATION

⊕ HUMANMIX—Indicates a mix of human beings.

① THE GENDERSPHERE—Distinguishes females from males.

◖ THE LEFT HEMI-GENDERSPHERE—Represents the female human.

◧ THE SHADED LEFT HEMI-GENDER-SPHERE—Tells age of female.

◖ THE UNSHADED LEFT HEMI-GENDER-SPHERE—Indicates a female child or virgin.

◙ THE EXED LEFT HEMI-GENDER-SPHERE—Female, of undetermined age or experience.

◖ THE RODDED LEFT HEMI-GENDER-SPHERE—One rod means single. Two rods means married. Three rods means divorced or widowed. No rods means information not available.

◗ THE RIGHT HEMI-GENDERSPHERE—Represents the male human.

♨ HORNS—Person is in high state of lust.

♨♨ WINGS—One wing means gay. Two wings means bisexual. No wings means heterosexual.

EXERCISES

It was a great party. Everyone was mixing it up and the repartee was flowing fast and heavy.

?"Hey, Daryl, do you see what I see."

"Yeah, Rock, she's a real beauty."

?"How old do you make her, Daryl."

?"I dunno, Rock. ?What difference does it make."

"I'm going to say something to her."

"Do it, Rock."

?"Uh, pardon me, young lady, but don't I recognize you from my judo class."

"Rock, it's me, Pancake."

?"Pancake. ?What are you doing here. I didn't know it was you for a moment."

"Rock, this is my friend Greeneyes."

"Nice to meet you, Greeneyes. ?Excuse me for asking, but isn't that an unusual name, Greeneyes."

"Well, yes, Rock, it is. You see, I was named after my great-aunt on my mother's side."

?"Is that right. Uh, Pancake and Greeneyes, this is my friend Daryl."

"Hello, Daryl."

"Pleased to meet you, ladies. But, Pancake, I already know you."

"Yes, you do, Daryl. But it's good to see you again."

?"Who's the little girl over there, Pancake."

"That's my little cousin, Rawasa. She's staying with us for a few days. I thought she'd enjoy the party."

"I'm glad I saw you, Pancake. And I'm glad I saw you too, Greeneyes."

"Likewise."

Later:

?"Daryl, who's that guy over there in the bat costume trying to hit on Pancake and Greeneyes."

"I don't know, Rock, but I don't think you have to worry."

?"Oh yeah. Well, I worry about everybody, Daryl. That's how come I got as far as I got."

"Rock, I think Pancake is signaling you."

?"Yeah. Hi, Pancake. ?What's up."

?"How about you and Daryl coming with me and Greeneyes for some hot cocoa after the party, Rock."

"That would be great, Pancake. ?But what about Batman and the little cousin."

"Don't worry, Rock. Batman is a dancer who is giving Rawasa lessons in tap. He promised to bring Rawasa back to my house after the party. Everything's fine, Rock. You worry too much."

"That's how I got as far as I got, Pancake."

"Hey, Daryl."

5

THE PUNCTUATION
OF FEAR AND
ANXIETY

This chapter will deal with the punctuation of fear, from deep panic to mild apprehension. Fear, in fact, may be our most pervasive emotion. Virtually nobody goes untouched by it in one form or another. BOO! Even here in the middle of a book on punctuation, you are not safe from it. Yet all too often feelings of fear go unacknowledged in standard prose, and unread. Perhaps it is the subtlety of the fear that the author can't quite capture with words, or the magnitude. Indeed, while the words of a given narrative may tell you whether the fear arises from a rhino charging or whether it is just a mouse under the table, they probably won't convey the degree of fear experienced by the subject, at least not without going into great elaboration. Fright signs, however, panic marks, startles, and yeeks (not to mention degree marks—see Chapter 3) will take care of most situations. No need for embarrassing confessionals. Metapunctuation to the rescue.

4 FRIGHT SIGNS

Of all the fear signs, fright signs are the ones most frequently encountered. They can be used to describe any of a myriad of garden-variety fears, such as fear of failure, fear of parental rebuke, fear of spiders, fear of public speaking. They are mild and can be dispensed liberally, alone or in multiples, depending on the situation. Thus if someone is experiencing simple apprehension over an upcoming exam, a single fright mark might do. Whereas if one was really scared—say that he was going to be expelled from school for plagiarizing or because he was being chased by a ghoul through a cemetery at night—two or three fright signs might be appropriate to indicate the intensity of fear. Fright signs, then, are quite common, and must be distinguished from deep terror, panic marks, yeeks, startles, and phobic brackets.

ϟ "The water looks cold."

ϟ ?"Are you sure this is the principal's office."

ϟ "I don't like the looks of it."

ϟ "I hope he doesn't call on me."

ϟ "Boy, this sure is high."

ϟ ?"What if I get caught."

The examples above are all simple fears easily denoted with single fear marks. On the other hand, the following examples might take two or three fear marks, or even more, to really make clear the fright felt.

ϟϟ "Yowee, Rock, that's a huge web."

𝄪 ?"I have to speak before both houses of Congress."

𝄪𝄪 ?"Did you say they found out that we transferred two billion dollars from the main office into our personal accounts."

𝄪𝄪 "I've never leaped from a moving jet without a parachute before."

𝄪𝄪 "Look, I'm hanging by my fingertips from the ledge of the eighty-fifth floor. ?Do you think someone could toss me a rope, or pull me in."

𝄪 !"I hear a noise downstairs, Daryl."

PANIC MARKS

Panic marks are quite different from fear signs. Panic marks are used when something precipitates a sudden and uncontrollable rush of adrenaline, causing the individual to lose control. The person "freaks," if you will, and loses his ability to cope, at least for the moment. Panic marks capture this interesting phenomenon with accuracy and understanding. When panic continues unabated for an extended time, or when the individual suffers continual or unending bouts of panic, the situation may call for phobic brackets. For the nonce we will deal with panic marks.

∨∕?"What is that, Daryl. Omigod, it's a snake. I think I'm going to faint."

∨∕"Rock, don't push me. I'll jump, just wait a moment."

∨∕"I know it's only an exam, but if I mess up these SATs, I won't get into the college of my choice. My parents will be humiliated. My life will be ruined, if not over. Dang, only twelve minutes left, and six hundred and ninety problems to go. I can't think, I can't think."

∨∕"Sure, go ahead, take my money, take my clothes, anything you want. Just don't shoot."

∨∕?"Why do I have to get undressed in front of the class."

∨∕"Three o'clock in the morning, only four hours left to get some sleep. C'mon, sleep, c'mon. Maybe if I count sheep. . . . But I hate sheep."

{ }   PHOBIC BRACKETS

Phobic brackets are usually used when enclosing an entire phobic episode or a series of thoughts that constitute an escalating phobic situation. Thus one of the examples used above, when extended, might properly call for phobic brackets.

{"Damn, it's three o'clock in the morning and I've got to make that important presentation today. I can't sleep. Only four hours left. If I don't get some sleep, I'll be a wreck, strung out. I'll feel lousy, won't be able to work. I'll mess up the presentation. The boss will notice and mark it against me. He hates me anyway. He'll probably threaten to fire me. If I lose my job, I'll be finished. I haven't got the strength to look for another job, not now. Darn it. C'mon, sleep, I've got to sleep."}

This example benefits from phobic brackets, which clearly state the degree of panic felt and isolate the episode within the text. They reinforce the sense of despair being experienced by the person trying to go to sleep and contain the escalating chain of thoughts so typical of the phobic situation.

Phobic brackets may also be used at any time in place of panic marks or in conjunction with panic marks to further emphasize the mounting loss of control and attending fear.

{"But I can't swim. I'll drown. ∨ !Help, help. !Blub, blub. Help, help."}

YEEKS

While at first glance yeeks may seem identical to startles (see below), they are actually quite different. Yeeks are used in situations when a person is not only startled but frightened. For example:

ᨓ?"What the hell kind of animal is that."

Here, yeeks preceding the sentence tell us that the person is not only startled, but also taken aback by the sheer ugliness of the animal or by the unreality of it. Perhaps it is an animal he has never seen before. Or perhaps one he has not seen in the snarling mode. In either event, yeeks will properly denote his feelings.

ᨓ!"Whoa. There's another one. They're all over the place. Let's get out of here."

ᨓ   YIKES

Yikes are just large yeeks, which are used when greater emphasis is called for. A yike can grow to any size, if appropriate.

ᨒ   STARTLES

Startles are used in instances of mild or sudden surprise. They do not carry with them the degree of shock or fear that yeeks or yikes do. Startles often produce soft smiles, as when the individual is amused by the surprise.

ᨒ"Oh, it's you, Harriet, heh, heh, heh."

ᨒ?"Three pounds is rather large for a goldfish, wouldn't you say."

))) "It's just the wind."

))) "Rover, don't jump on me like that."

)))?"Am I hearing things, or is that parakeet singing 'Home on the Range.'"

))) "That's not beef. That's vegetable rind."

))) "Button your fly, Harvey."

● DEEP TERROR OR FEAR UNTO DEATH

One of the most horrible of all emotions, deep terror or fear unto death, should be marked accordingly and used reservedly. While it is possible that someone could feel deep terror visiting the dentist, it is more often saved for life threats or, at the very least, perceived life threats. Thus the mortal fear Pauline probably experiences on the approach of a train, knowing she is tied to the train tracks, could quite properly be described as deep terror and should be so denoted. Further examples:

●!"No, no, no, no, aieeeeee, aargh."

●"!But I can't swim."

●?"What are you going to do with me. ?Why are you putting me in this cauldron of boiling water, ow, ouch, yow."

♠ "Jack, the pilot is throwing up in the bathroom. You have to fly the plane."

♠ ?"What are all these little fish around here. ?Piranhas, did you say."

♠ ?"Your husband's home."

♠ ?"Did you say the tuna fish tested positive for botulism. But I just ate an entire can."

♠ ?"Me, fight Mike Tyson. ?*Moi*. Let go of me. I don't want to, I said I don't want to. I never called him a wimp, I swear."

♠ !"Hurry, hurry. I'm barely holding on. It's an eighty-five-floor drop. !Hurry. !My fingers are slipping, slipping, ohoooooooooooooooooooooooooo."

♠ I'm afraid this chapter's over—except for the exercise.

SYMBOL SUMMARY

THE PUNCTUATION OF FEAR AND ANXIETY

⚡ FRIGHT SIGNS—Used to describe any of a myriad of garden-variety fears, such as fear of failure or fear of spiders. They can be used singly or multiply.

\/ PANIC MARKS—Indicates a person is "freaking" and losing control.

{ } PHOBIC BRACKETS—Used to enclose an entire phobic episode.

Ⱳ YEEKS—Used when someone is both frightened and startled.

Ⱳ YIKES—Large yeeks, when greater emphasis is called for.

)) STARTLES—Indicate mild but sudden surprise.

● DEEP TERROR OR FEAR UNTO DEATH—Saved for the most horrible of emotions.

EXERCISES

?"Rock, do you really think camping out on this island is a good idea."

"I wish you weren't such a lily liver, Daryl. We're gonna have a great time."

"I know, Rock. It's just that it's getting dark and this cave you chose to sleep in is pretty spooky."

?"What's spooky, Daryl. ?A few cobwebs. ?A few bats. C'mon, Daryl, you and I have been in street wars together."

"Yeah, I know, Rock, but this is different. ?What was that."

?"What was what, Daryl."

?"Didn't you hear a woooo woooo sound."

"No, I didn't hear any woooo woooo sound, Daryl."

"Sorry, Rock. ?Woweee, what's that in the corner."

"Easy, Daryl. That's a little racoon."

"That racoon is climbing up the web, Rock."

"Jeez, you're right, Daryl. That's some kind of giant spider. Let's get out of here."

!"Rock. !Rock. I'm caught in a web."

"Stay calm, Daryl. I've got a knife, I'll cut you out."

!"Hurry, Rock, hurry."

"I'm cutting, Daryl. Relax."

"Omigod, Rock, it's one of those giant spiders coming toward us."

?"Where, Daryl, where."

"Right behind you, Rock."

!"Yow."

"Rock, Rock, c'mon back. I'm still in the web."

"Jump, Daryl, jump."

?"What do you mean jump, Rock. ?How can I jump. Help, Rock, help."

"I'll go for help, Daryl. Don't worry."

"Don't go, Rock. There's no one on the island but us. Help me. Cut me loose. Hurry, Rock, hurry."

!"Aieeeee. Something just bit me. I'm bit, Daryl, I'm bit."

"Nothing bit you, Rock. That was a stick you backed into. Now get me out of this web, quick. Please, Rock."

"Okay, Daryl, you're out. Now let's get out of here."

"Watch it, Rock, watch it, you're running into another web."

!"@#&*!!*."

"Step on that one, Daryl. I've got this one. !Yikes. It's a big one."

"I can't take it, Rock. I'm running for it."

"No, Daryl. Don't leave me. Wait for me, I'm right behind you."

"I can't wait, Rock. I'm running for it."

!"Wait, Daryl, wait."

"Into the boat, quick."

"I'm in. Let's get out of here. Hurry."

"Holy smoke, Daryl, there's one in the back of the boat."

?"A spider, Rock."

"Yeah, a huge one."

"That's not a spider, Rock. That's my jacket."

"Sure looks like a spider to me."

6

THE PUNCTUATION OF LOVE AND HATE

LOVE

Love marks, and I don't mean those little bites and bruises left on the necks and thighs of lovers, constitute one of the most important families of signs in communication notation. How often do we hear people say, "Words can't express how I feel about you." Remember Christian in *Cyrano de Bergerac*? He was an admirable soldier, articulate even, but when it came to his feelings of love for Roxanne, he became tongue-tied, and Cyrano had to speak for him. Many people are like Christian. They cannot express their true feelings, especially about love. Sometimes they can't express them because they don't understand them. Other times they understand them but can't articulate them. Even authors, who should know their own characters well, have difficulty putting into words how a character is feeling, his internal emotions. But when the author does understand how he wants a character to feel, he should make it clear to the reader. Metapunctuation will help the author accomplish that end.

Naturally, as with any complex emotion, love comes in many forms. It often comes unbidden, like a tropical storm, hot and tempestuous, causing general havoc and disarray, then leaves as suddenly as it came. Sometimes it simply reflects the gradual deepening of affection between friends that goes unnoticed until one day it is just there. Love may be sexual and all-consuming, a fire that rages inside and out until it is extinguished or at least controlled. Love may be platonic, combining the most beautiful elements of respect, admiration, reverence, and deep friendship. It may occur between males and females, between members of the same sex, between family members, and between humans and their pets. Often it is seen in the wings, waiting to come out, beckoning doctor and patient, teacher and student, employee and employer, tempting them to taste of its titillations and seductions. It rearranges priorities and hopes among young people and old, among fat people and thin, among rich people and poor, among intelligent persons and those less gifted. It flourishes despite color barriers, religious barriers, philosophical barriers, parental and political restrictions, self-doubt, and dozens of other obstacles. Nothing can stop it. Surely, then, such a pervasive and formidable entity deserves some special handling in written text.

Metapunctuation tries to accommodate love's special needs—its distinguishing marks, characteristics, and shadings.

=   ATTRACTS

Before romantic love, infatuation, passion, or flirtation can take place, there is attraction, that indefinable something that pulls two individuals toward one another—a mutual magnetism that draws them ineluctably together. Sometimes the attraction is unidirectional, where only one of the parties is attracted to the other. This can lead to unrequited love or, as in the film, a fatal attraction, but it begins as attraction. Clearly it is important to indicate when attraction is taking place, for it will color any situation and is worthy of the reader's attention.

In metapunctuation, attraction is indicated by attracts, which look like equal signs but are used like quotation marks to enclose a period of active attraction.

= "Nice to meet you, Rock."=
= "Nice to meet you too— ?Pancake. What a great name."=

= ?"Who is that magnificence standing over there in the corner looking my way."=
He glanced in her direction.
= ?"Haven't I seen you somewhere before—like in my dreams."=

When attraction is unreciprocated—a one-way street—only one attract is used. It is placed before the words of the speaker who is feeling the attraction.

⇌ ?"Well, how are you, gorgeous."

?"Where did you get that line, out of a grade Q movie."

⇌ "Sorry, I meant no offense."

"No offense taken. Well, I've got to go now."

⇌ "Please don't go. My name's Daryl."

⧺ FATAL ATTRACTION

Rare instances of fatal attractions are indicated either by a single attract sign with a dagger through it or, in mutual attractions, by a pair of attracts with a dagger through the one who feels the fatal attraction.

⧺ "Yes, you are certainly my type of man."

⇌ ?"May I call you this evening, Pancake."

⧺ "Please do, Rock."

⧺ "So, you thought you could avoid me. Well, I'm not so easily disposed of."

♡ ROMANTIC LOVE

Nothing quite compares to romantic love, the kind that knocks you off your feet and causes your heart to race and your mind to dream endlessly about the object of your love. For those in love, the world is suddenly transformed into one of bright light and endless possibilities. Nothing is too great or so daunting that it would keep you from obtaining your desires. A single encouraging glance from your loved one is enough to make you mount your steed and ride triumphantly up the highest mountain or across the widest plain. You feel unaccountably like bursting into song and smiling for no reason at all. Hidden harps and symphonic music accompany your every action.

This kind of exhilarating and heightened state of being, sometimes called "hysteroid dysphoria," deserves to be specifically designated and communicated so that others reading about it can properly understand and appreciate temporary lapses and aberrations in behavior. It is true that most people love a lover, someone bewitched by romantic love, but not if they can't recognize the lover when they see him or her. Metapunctuation, using romantic love hearts, tries to isolate and distinguish the person romantically in love.

♡"No, it's okay if you walk across my face. I don't mind."

♡?"Isn't it a beautiful day."
   "But it's raining."
♡?"Yes, don't you just love rain."

♡"I feel like jumping and dancing."
   ?"Are you all right. ?Did you take anything I should know about."
♡"No, I'm just fine. Da, da, da, da, dada."

♡?"Only twenty of them, eh. I will vanquish them in the twinkling of an eye."

"You're wearing one brown shoe and one black shoe."
♡?"Is that so. ?What do you know. So I am."

♡?"Good morning, Mrs. Ference, and how are you today?"

♡?"Ten dollars. Here, take fifty dollars."

♡?"Why am I smiling. I don't know why I'm smiling."

♡   **INFATUATION MARKS**

Infatuation, no matter how foolishly based, is difficult to distinguish from romantic love, especially for the person afflicted. It has many of the same characteristics. Infatuated persons are obsessed with the object of their love. They sing songs, hear music, and dream fantasies, seldom recognizing either the unworthiness of their love or its evanescence. Often it is not until after their ardor has cooled down that infatuated persons recognize that they have only been infatuated and not truly in love. Thus it becomes terribly important to distinguish infatuation from true romantic love whenever possible. Authors often know when characters are merely infatuated and not forever-until-the-end-of-time in love. It is important for readers to know also. Infatuation marks help us distinguish between these loves.

⬦"I'm in love, I'm in love, I'm in love."

"But Daryl, she's already married to six other men."

⬦"She's beautiful. You're a fool. I'm in love."

⬦"I love you, Annabelle."

⬦"I love you too, Edgar."

⬦"Let's get married in this kingdom by the sea."

⬦"We can't, Edgar. I'm only twelve, and in New York you have to be eighteen."

⬦"Did you see that physique? I can't stand it. I'm in love. I'm going to marry him."

"But Pancake, you haven't even met him yet. He doesn't know who you are."

⬦"That's okay, I'm in love. I'm going to get married."

⬦?"What do you mean, you're a preoperative transexual, Pancake. ?Does this mean I can't marry you, that you're not a woman. ?That you can't have our children."

⬦"Well, not yet, Rock, Snookums, but with modern medicine, maybe one day."

!"Aieeeeeeee."

❖ LUST DUST

Sprinkles of dots in loose formation signify down-and-dirty sexual lust. There is no dancing around this emotion, no dissembling and pretending higher aims. Lust is basic and instinctual. It is raw hunger that cries out for satisfaction.

❖ !"Will you look at those buns. !Holy cow. I'm in love."

He who has not experienced lust at one time or another is probably without glands. Even proper and highborn ladies experience lust. It is basic and hormonal, primitive but universal. True, some people seem more successful than others at keeping lust at bay, locked up and controlled, but in most healthy human beings, it is there just waiting to emerge. Sometimes in the most awkward settings.

❖ !"Arrrrgh. I want you. Now, here, on the ground."
❖ "But Jimmy, my parents and friends and schoolmates are all standing over there, watching."
❖ ?"Watching, eh. Good, that turns me on."

Lust has a simplicity about it that is refreshing. It is direct and honest.

❖ "Me Tarzan, you Jane. !Aieeeooooouuu-ooouuu."

And you always thought Tarzan was giving a victory cry. If only Edgar Rice Burroughs had known about metapunctuation. Perhaps you would have read those jungle books with an amplified understanding.

❖!"Aieeeooooooouuuooouuu."

With lust dust, you might read:

❖ "She had a high forehead, blond hair, and dimples. I took her to be a lady through and through."

But you would know the protagonist really was saying he wanted to take Little Bo Peep for a roll in the hay. And why not? Little Bo Peep was giving off lust dust as well. She was just quieter about expressing it.

Of course, as with any metapunctuation, lust dust can be used in conjunction with other notation, for example:

❖ ♡"I suppose the thing I love most about her is her incredible body. True, her 180 IQ is attractive too, and her sense of humor, but that body is, ?how do you say in English, !'Ummmmmvavavooom.' "

Here the individual may genuinely be experiencing romantic love or infatuation or some emotion of the heart, but lust is also present and must be indicated so that proper inflections, gestures, and expressions can be used.

There are times when words give few signals as to what is actually going on, and only the presence of lust dust will convey the meaning of the moment.

❖ "Hi, my name's Jerry."

Jerry may be a satyr in full flame, with horns and drool, but unless the words go on to further description, the image is lost. Lust dust saves the day.

❖ The construction workers were sitting on the sidewalk, next to each other, when Janet walked by.

Now it is conceivable that these gentlemen might just be having higher thoughts, about the nature of man, cosmology, or the British system of jurisprudence, when Janet walks by. Sorry, the lust dust rising above the words means you were right, they are *not* thinking about the nature of man, cosmology, or the British justice system. Whatever possessed me?

∃ **FLIRTS**

Flirts are little lines curving to the left, in pairs or groups, that indicate flirting is taking place. Flirting, the act of engaging another individual in coy sexual invitation, usually with courtship in mind, is universal. It is done with facial expressions, body gestures, winking, verbal exchanges, and even physical transactions. Sometimes it is obvious, sometimes not. Sometimes intentional, sometimes not. Sometimes the act of flirting is so subtle as to elude even the flirtee. This is when punctuation flirts become especially important. Punctuation flirts prepare the reader for what is going on even when the flirtee is ignorant of the situation. Now the reader has a better understanding of what is transpiring and is able to communicate this understanding to listeners, or to himself, as the case may be.

$\Im$?"So you're into iron maidens, are you, Pancake. !You little devil."

$\Im$?"Good dip, Rock, don't you think."

$\Im$?"I just love parties, Pancake, don't you."

$\Im$"Yeah, Rock, me too."

$\Im$"You have great eyes, Pancake."

$\Im$"Thank you, Rock, your eyes are pretty good yourself, you know."

$\Im$"I love iron maidens, Pancake. You don't have to be embarrassed."

I am aware that some grammarians might ask what an iron maiden is, but we won't get into that.

Sometimes flirting may seem like anything but flirting. Children, for example, flirt roughly.

ƺ"You pushed me."
ƺ"!Yeah. And I'll push you again."

Most adults would not recognize this exchange as flirting, but it is.

ƺ"You took my inkwell, Bobby. Give it back."
ƺ"No, you'll have to try and get it."

Kids flirt differently from adults. Of course, these are youngsters from my memory banks a hundred years ago—inkwells? And gangsters flirt differently from other people, and so do physicists. In fact, most people have methods of flirting that reflect their personal style—many of which go unrecognized. Metapunctuation flirts, therefore, are very important. They send up flags. They are like typographical pheromones. Which brings us to heat.

Often in situations of flirting and especially of lust, and certainly in anger, degrees of heat become useful. They tell us just how hot a situation is, how passionate individuals are. Teens today even describe attractive members of the other sex as "hot." Heat degrees are represented by little superscript o's just as they are in temperature readings. See Chapter 3 for further explanation.

Lust dust, flirts, and heat degrees really tell us a great deal—don't you think? We would all operate better if we had access to such markers in actual life situations. Alas, these are reserved for the printed page.

❡   **INVERTED PLATONIC DROPS**

When you see inverted platonic drops or tears before a sentence, you know platonic love is present. Originally discussed by Plato (full discussion in the *Symposium*)—hence the eponymy—platonic love represents the reverential love a student may feel for his teacher or mentor. It is usually nonsexual, often spiritual and deeply felt. It exists also between friends who are not lovers, just friends. It is special and strong. It needs to be represented. In metapunctuation, it is represented by inverted platonic drops.

❡?"Mr. Johnson, could I take a moment of your time."

❡"Hildebrand is the best teacher I ever had."

❡?"You mean a great deal to me, Margaret, but how shall I say this. I love you, truly, but I don't want to sleep with you."

❡"Jackie, you are my best friend. I love you."

❡"He is the most wonderful man I have ever met."

〰 PASSION WAVES

Passion is different from lust in that it also implies power and motion. People make love passionately. People feel passionately about things and causes. People are moved by passion. The distinction is fine, but it is there. Passion is represented in metapunctuation by waves.

〰!"Oh. I love you, Cindy. !Oh. !Ooooh. I could eat you up."

〰!"Never will I give up my belief that chocolate is the great healer, do you hear me, never, never."

〰"I can't wait to get my hands on her."

〰"I want it so bad I can taste it."

〰"I will do it if it kills me."

〰"I love what I do. Never have I been happier. It is the best decision I ever made."

〰"There is only one way to make good French toast as far as I am concerned, and that is to use Pepperidge Farm bread, soak it in eggs with no other adornments, and fry it in butter. Any other way is a compromise."

〰!"Long live Filbert. !Long live the king."

〰"Do it, David, do it."

≠   NOT EQUAL SIGN

In mathematics, the not equal sign tells us that two numbers or amounts are unequal. In relationships, especially love relationships, the not equal sign tells us the love is one-sided.

Unfortunately in romantic love, inequality is often the rule. Individuals fall hopelessly in love with other individuals only to discover ultimately that the other individual doesn't give a hoot, or cares for the first in a platonic way. Nothing is sadder. Sometimes if a badly broken heart is involved, the not equal sign may be replaced by a broken heart to illustrate the severity of the unrequited love. When you see a broken heart, great sympathy is called for.

♡"But you told me you loved me, Rock."

≠?"What did he say, Marigold. ?Did he say he even noticed me."

≠"Let me put it this way, Daryl. I like you, but I don't love you."

≠"There he is. I can't believe it, Marigold !It's him, eeeeeeh."

≠"Let me be your doormat. I am yours to command."

≠!"Okay, lie down."

HATE

Everyone hates. Hating is an extreme emotion that helps us vent our pent-up frustrations and distastes. It is cathartic. Even giving voice to what we hate helps us feel better. We hate dust, we hate working on weekends, we hate people who say nasty things about us, we hate rivals, we hate anxiety, we hate prune yogurt, we hate liver, we hate spiders, and we especially hate you, Jerry!

But there is a difference between hating Jerry and hating to sweep up. Between hating liver and hating crass and lurid advertisements. There is also a difference in the depth of our hatred for these various people and things. All of this ocean of hatred must be sorted out for the reader if he is to communicate clearly and effectively. Wars have been started because of hatred, and sometimes because of mistaken perceptions of hatred. Certainly relationships have been ended because of hatred. Hatred is an important emotion, one that needs to be handled carefully and signaled clearly. Metapunctuation will help with these functions.

†† DAGGERS

Daggers, usually in pairs, are used to indicate intense hatred of another person, such that the hater would like to kill the hatee. Given the opportunity, the hater would gladly grab the punctuational daggers that mark his hatred in print and plunge them into the person he hates.

††!"Take this, Jack, you two-timing sonofabitch bastard lowlife."

††"He is the scum of the earth. I'd like to see him fry in hell."

††"Not only would I like to kill her, I'd like to do it with my own hands."

◖◗ DOUBLE VENOM DROPS

Double venom drops are used to express poisonous hatred for someone. It is usually a hatred that is seething under the surface, more in the wish stage than in the active loathing stage. Often venom drops are used in conjunction with a delta sarc mark.

◖◗"I do wish him well in all that he attempts."

◖◗"She's just a darling."

🌢🌢?"Pancake, eh. ?How do I feel about Pancake."

🌢🌢?"School. Oh, school is great."

As you can see, these sentences can be read in a variety of ways. Double venom drops let the reader know exactly where the speaker stands.

╲╲ LINES OF LOATHING

Loathing is a deep or intense hatred for someone or something. Lines of loathing used in conjunction with daggers or venom drops are often used to underscore the depth and intensity of negative feeling.

╲"That scoundrel actually took my last dollar."

╲"His political instincts are just like those of his mentor, the boa constrictor at the Bronx Zoo."

╲?"Do I have strong feelings about blackmail. ?Is that what you want to know."

ﮩ SCORNS

Scorns, little horns curling to the left, usually appearing singly or in pairs depending on strength of feeling, denote contempt for the object at hand. Thus someone who has just stolen candy from the proverbial baby might be described with scorns attending.

ᴣᴣ"That guy just stole Snookum's candy."

ᴣᴣ?"He stole candy from two hundred babies all in the same day. That's sick."

ᴣᴣ"I don't believe in free speech. People who talk openly about boiling down fat people for their lard should be shut up."

ᴣᴣ"Anyone who would mock his own country is not someone I wish to be law partners with."

℅   CONTEMPTO DRIPS

Contempto drips reflect ultimate disdain or contempt for a person or action.

℅"This guy is the most despicable character I have ever met."

℅"He's the one responsible for my being fired."

℅"Yes, he ran off with my first three wives, that's true."

℅?"Ron Dumond. ?Ron Dumond. ?Ron Doooomonnd."

SYMBOL SUMMARY

THE PUNCTUATION OF LOVE AND HATE

= ATTRACTS—That which precedes love, infatuation, passion, or flirtation.

‡ FATAL ATTRACTION—Dangerous attraction.

♡ ROMANTIC LOVE—Indicates the genuine article, the kind that knocks your socks off.

◊ INFATUATION MARKS—Indicates early love or maybe a crush.

∴ LUST DUST—Indicates raw sexual hunger.

Ƹ FLIRTS—Indicates that one individual or both are engaging in coy sexual invitation.

❙ INVERTED PLATONIC DROPS—Platonic love.

〰 PASSION WAVES—Indicates power and motion.

≠ NOT EQUAL SIGN—One love is greater than the other.

♥ BROKEN HEART—Expresses intensity of unrequited love.

†† DAGGERS—Indicates intense hatred.

🌢 DOUBLE VENOM DROPS—Expresses poisonous hatred.

⟍ LINES OF LOATHING—Expresses deep, intense hatred.

ﻬ SCORNS—Indicates contempt or scorn.

℗ CONTEMPTO DRIPS—Expresses complete disdain and contempt for a person or action.

EXERCISES

?"Hi, Rock, how's it goin'."

"Uh, oh great, Lily. ?Who's that gorgeous thing over there."

"That's Jenny the Crab, Rock. She's a tramp."

?"Jenny the Crab, eh. She's got some pair of claws on her."

"Easy, Rock. Pancake's in the other room."

"Yeah, I know. Don't worry about me and Pancake."

"Touchy, touchy, Rock."

"Get lost, Lily."

"Hi, baby. ?Can you move sideways."

"I don't know, handsome. ?What do you have in mind."

?"Aren't you Jenny the Crab."

"Well, that's what they call me."

"You kind of turn me on."

"You kind of turn me on too."

"Uh, oh, here comes Pancake."

?"Who are you flirting with, Rock."

"Uh, no one, Pancake."

"Don't lie to me, Rock. ?You were flirting with that crab tramp, weren't you. Everyone knows she's called Jenny the Crab because that's what you'll get from her."

"Pancake, honey, you got me wrong."

"Rock, I know you like the back of my hand."

Later:

"Hey, Jenny. It's me, Rock. ?How about you and me going out for a drink."

"Get lost, Rock. You're with Pancake."

"Not really. Just sometimes."

"You're a flake, Rock. Beat it."

"But you really do it for me, baby."

"Rock, take a walk, before I call some friends to have you tossed out."

"C'mon, Jenny. I like your style."

"Rock, you're beginning to get on my nerves. Now take the hint. Get lost."

Much later:

"Daryl, I can't seem to get Jenny the Crab out of my mind."

"You're just thinking sex, Rock."

"I don't know, Daryl. She does something to me."

"Leave her alone, Rock."

"I'm going to follow her home tonight. If she's seeing that creep Roger . . ."

"Rock, drop her. Forget her. She's nothing but trouble. Trust me."

"I can't stand the thought of that Roger taking her home."

"Rock, let's go to a movie."

"I'll see you later, Daryl."

Next day:

"Hey, Rock, you poor sap. ?You got a thing for Jenny, eh."

"Stick it, Roger. I couldn't care less about Jenny. She deserves a dork like you."

"Na na na, Rock. You sound a little jealous."

?"Me jealous of you, Roger. Ha. That's rich."

"I love you too, Rock. ?Just stay away from Jenny, you hear."

"Don't tell me what I can do and what I can't, Roger. I do what I want, when I want. Now move the hell out of my way."

"No need to get nasty, jerk. See you around."

7

TYPE EMPHASIS AND CONVERTED MUSICAL NOTATION

TYPE EMPHASIS

Simply put, we use type not only to indicate shades up and down but also to directly control loudness and softness. #9, for example, represents a whisper; #12, normal speech tones; and #24, stentorian bellows. Let's begin with #9.

#9 point—A whisper. Shhhh, don't say it too loud, we wouldn't want the others to hear.

?"What was that, Mabel."
"I said he looks like a gorilla."

#10 point—A hushed tone, slightly louder than a whisper.

?"Where are you, Jack."
"Over here behind the flamingo cage."

#12 point—Normal tones.

"So this is how it looks. !Terrific."

"Jerry went to the movies."

#14 point—Rather louder than normal tones.

"Look, Pete, I'm not going."

!"Hey. Way to go."

#18 point—Loud.

"Over here."

?"Can you hear me, Max."

!"Lean to the left, lean to the right, stand up, sit down, fight, fight, fight."

#24 point—Stentorian.

"I'm sorry I don't have a microphone, but I'll try to make

even those across the street hear me."

"Throw, you idiot, throw the ball."

"I'll shout it so the whole world will hear. !I love you, I LOVE YOU."

CONVERTED MUSICAL NOTATION

Music and language are closely related—both offer meaning through sound; both have rhythms, cadences, and tonality; and both depend on modulations, pitch, inflections, etc. Therefore, it is natural that many of the notations of music, especially those having to do with rhythm, pacing, etc., would be useful for language. Language, after all, is full of music, and vice versa.

For metapunctuation, I have borrowed a number of musical notations originally intended as visual instructions for performers and have converted or adapted them for language. They already exist, they work wonderfully for music, and hence they will work wonderfully for language.

With the converted musical notation, it is perfectly all right simply to write the direction above or below the sentence or paragraph where it applies. Or you may use the symbol notation if you prefer. Musical notation thus becomes part of the new metalanguage. Also, the term "perform," for the purposes of metapunctuation, should be understood to mean the manner in which you read.

⌐ Accelerando (Italian)—A direction to speed up gradually. ?What could be more useful. So often we are called upon to speed up what we are saying, either for a short run or a longer play.

♩!"C'mon baby, c'mon baby, let's go, atta baby, atta baby, way to go, way to go—c'mon you've got it, you've got it, yeahhhhh."

♩ Quietly he crept into the house, then on approaching the room where they were all sleeping, he began to move swiftly, grabbing the chalice, turning on the lights, shouting to confuse them, then running as fast as he could in all directions at once.

♩ The drumbeats came slowly at first, pounding out a rhythmic message. Then they began to quicken. Faster and faster they came until they seemed almost one continuous drone, faster and faster still, louder and louder, faster and faster, until his head seemed as if it would burst.

♑ Adagio (Italian)—A slow tempo, slower than andante but faster than largo.

♑ The tintinnabulation of the bells, bells, bells, bells, the ringing and the singing of the bells, bells, bells, bells (or however Poe wrote it in "The Bells").

☺ Adagissimo (Italian)—A very slow tempo.

∪∪∪ Affabile (Italian)—A direction to perform in a smooth, graceful manner.

∪∪∪ "Come here, darling. That's it, I'm not going to hurt you."

🗲Allargando (Italian)—A direction to slow down, and usually to perform with increased loudness.

🗲"Fi, fi, fo, fum, I smell the blood of an Englishman."

〰️Allegro (Italian)—A fast tempo, faster than andante, but not as fast as presto. Originally meant cheerful, joyful.

〰️"I'm so happy I could sing."

〰️"In the merry merry month of May, I was taken by surprise, by a pair of roguish eyes . . . ."

〰️"This is terrific. I'm so excited I can hardly contain myself."

o•o•oAndante (Italian)—A moderate tempo, faster than adagio, but slower than allegro.

♞Angstlich (German)—A direction to perform in an anxious, fearful manner.

♞"As I walked through the woods, my heart was in my mouth."

♞"I don't like spiders, and feeling my way blindly through this cave with its giant webs gave me the willies."

♞"Please don't shoot."

✦ Appassionato (Italian)—A direction to perform with intense feeling.

✦ "Jasmine, I love you more than I know how to say."

✦ "Roxanne, I love you more than I know how to say."

✦ "Trudy, I love you more than I know how to say."

✦ "Now is the time to strike."

✦ "I would give my life for the organization, believe me."

〰 Arioso (Italian)—A style of recitative that is more songlike and more expressive than an ordinary recitative.

〰 "Come here, Fifi, I know you're in there hiding."

〰 "Nice little girls don't drive a spike into their brother's head without provocation, Nanda."

〰 ?"Rock, Rock, what am I going to do with you, Rock."

⟶≫ Attacca (Italian)—"Attack." A direction at the end of a movement or section of a composition indicating that the next movement or section is to proceed immediately, without pause. In prose the same direction would hold true—to move on immediately to the next paragraph or section.

—≫ "And so it went."

—≫ "Now let's assume, for the sake of argument, that . . ."

♠ Bestimmt (German)—A direction to stress a note, phrase, or section. Obviously the same would apply to a word, phrase, or section.

♠ "You aggravating creature."

♠ "You, you're the love of my life."

♠ "Yes, you, over there in the corner trying to avoid my eye."

❀ Bewegt (German)—A direction to perform in a lively, animated manner.

❀ "All around the mulberry bush, the monkey chased the weasel . . ."

♀B Brilliante (Italian)—A direction to perform in a showy, brilliant manner. In metapunctuation this means to read in a showy, brilliant manner.

♀B Think of José Ferrer performing Cyrano de Bergerac.

‖ – Brusco (Italian)—A direction to perform in a brusque, abrupt manner, with harsh accents.

‖ – "!Be gone."

‖ – "I have nothing to say to you."

◊ Burlesco (Italian)—A direction to perform in a comical, jesting manner.

◊ "Slap me five, baby."

◊ "Lika this, anda that."

Burlesco would be appropriate when mimicking someone or parodying a style.

⌒ Calmando (Italian)—A direction to perform in a quiet, calm manner.

⌒ "There is no need to worry, Rebecca. I will help you."

⌒ "So the car smashed through the living room window. ?So what. We can always buy another window."

⌒ "As I read this, you close your eyes and try to fall asleep."

𝄋 Celere (Italian)—A direction to perform quickly.

🎶?"How much wood could a woodchuck chuck if a woodchuck could chuck wood."

🎶"As much wood as a woodchuck would chuck if a woodchuck could chuck wood."

O Chiaramente (Italian)—A direction to perform clearly and distinctly.

O "How now, brown cow, grazing in the green, green grass."

⋎ Delicato (Italian)—A direction to perform in a delicate, gentle, elegant manner.

⋎ Here and there one could see Christmas ornaments made of glistening spun glass, gossamer threads, and fine silks.

⋎ Gently he caressed her thighs, as if they were flower petals, urging them to open, yet never forcing them. In time they responded softly to his ministrations.

✳• Derb (German)—Direction to perform in a rough, bold manner.

✳•"Throw him in the brig."

✳•"I'm fed up with you animals. Get the hell out of here and don't come back."

♲ Diluendo (Italian)—A direction to perform more and more softly, until the sound literally fades away.

♲ In the distance his voice trailed off until only a faint echo remained.

♲ "You are becoming sleepy, very sleepy, sleepy, sleepy, that's it, sleepy, sleepy."

◖◖ Dolento or doloroso (Italian)—A direction to perform in a sorrowful manner.

◖◖ "Look, I can't stand it anymore. I love you, but you're driving me crazy."

◖◖?"God, did you see how he squashed that poor little creature."

◖◖ There is nothing more pitiful than an old person who has been cast out, shorn of any dignity, to fend for himself.

∿ Drammatico (Italian)—Direction to perform in a dramatic, slightly exaggerated manner.

∿ ?"Well, there, Percival, and how are you this evening."

◗ Duster (German)—Direction to perform in a gloomy, mournful manner.

⌒● "There lies Jack Spratt; alas, he could eat no more fat. And beside him his fat wife who used to lick the platter clean. Ah, it begrieves me to see them here."

─●─ Einfach (German)—Direction to perform in a simple, unadorned manner.

─●─ She was plain and simple. No frills nor fakery became her.

℀ Elegante (Italian)—Direction to perform in an elegant and stylish manner.

℀ The manner of this book.

\\ Emphatique (French)—To perform with emphasis and decision.

|||⟩ Encore (French)—Direction to repeat.

|||⟩ "One hundred bottles of beer on the wall, one hundred bottles of beer . . ."

▲ Entschlossen or entschieden (German)—A direction to perform in a decided, resolute manner.

▲ "Thus, today, I have instructed the chairman of the joint chiefs of staff to order our forces to attack Canada, because I believe that Canada has huge natural resources they aren't using and apparently aren't willing to share with us. This will teach them to share."

𝄐 Espressivo (Italian)—A direction to perform with expression, with feeling.

𝄐 "Ooooh, how I love you. I could eat you up."

> Estinto (Italian); also Etient (French)—A direction to perform as softly as possible.

> He tiptoed up the stairs, then, like a big happy ghost, blew open the door.

_∧ Fastoso (Italian)—Direction to perform in a dignified, stately manner.

_∧ "And now, it is my great pleasure to introduce Lord and Lady Windemere . . . Milord."

∧⁄ Feroce (Italian)—Direction to perform with vehemence and passion.

∧⁄ "Kill him, guys. Rip his throat out."

∧⁄ He gobbled her up as though she were a pastry rather than a lover.

𝄊 Fin al segno (Italian)—Signal that the performer is to repeat from the beginning to the sign.

♀"Lean to the left, lean to the right, stand up, sit down, fight, fight, fight."

⚡ Fortissimo (Italian)—Direction to perform very loudly.

⚡"Friends, Romans, and countrymen, lend me your ears."

⚡?"You up there in the blimp, can you hear me."

⚔ Furioso (Italian)—Direction to perform in a wild, passionate manner.

⚔"There, no, there, hurry, hurry, they'll be here any minute."

☋ Geheimnisvoll (German)—Direction to perform in a mysterious, secretive manner.

☋ Slowly he inched his way around the outside of the saucer. A cool, unearthly glow emanated from within, bathing the grounds in an eerie greenish yellow.

� Giocoso (Italian)—Direction to perform in a playful, gleeful manner.

⟩⟩• Heftig (German)—Direction to perform in a vehement, impetuous manner.

⇥• "Screw 'em, let's get on with it."

〰 Incalzanzo (Italian)—Direction to perform with increasing warmth and speed.

〰! "Oooh. I like the way you do that. Do it again, that's it, again, again."

Ⅴⅱ Indeciso (Italian)—Direction to perform in a hesitant, indecisive manner.

Ⅴⅱ ? "Yes, no. ?Shall we, no. ?Yes. ?What."

℘ Lusingando (Italian)—Direction to perform in a persuasive, coaxing manner.

℘ "Oh please, pretty please, pretty, pretty please."

ℳ Mormorando (Italian)—Direction to perform with a gentle, murmuring tone.

ℳ The wind was soughing through the trees.

☰| Mosso (Italian)—Direction to perform in a quick, agitated manner.

☰| "C'mon, Charlie, hurry up. We're late."

𝒩 Non (Italian)—Term meaning "not," as in allegro ma non troppo, "fast, but not too fast."

𝄫 "Ta ra ra boom de ay, ta ra ra boom de ay."

𝄪 Piano, pianissimo (Italian)—Directions to perform softly, and very softly.

⇑ Piu (Italian)—Term meaning "more," as in piu lento ("slower") or piu moto ("faster").

⇑ "They were coming at us, one at a time, then two at a time, then three at a time."

⁝ Poco (Italian)—Term meaning "little," as in un poco crescendo ("becoming slightly louder").

⁝ ?"What was that, Jack."

⁝ I said, ?"What time is it."

⇢ Pressando (Italian)—To perform with increasing speed.

⇢ "I know I can, I know I can, I know I can."

⇗ Prestissimo (Italian)—Direction to perform at the quickest possible tempo.

•|•|•| Rap—A kind of improvised chatter, often in rhyme, used to accompany reggae music, but also simply a chant or rhythm of speaking.

↙ Ritenuto (Italian)—Direction to hold back; to perform somewhat more slowly, but immediately, not gradually.

♪ "And now, let's relax."

⦅ Scherzando (Italian)—Direction to perform in a playful manner.

♪ Sospirando (Italian)—Direction to perform in a sighing, plaintive manner.

♪ "Damn, I can't believe it's happening again."

♪ "Oh, no, not again."

♪ Sotto voce (Italian)—Direction to perform in a low, whispering undertone.

♪! "Shhhh. There it is now. See if you can reach it."

♪ Staccato (Italian)—Direction to perform quickly and lightly.

♪ "First you, then him, then me, then Carol, then Julie, then you again."

♪ Tacet (Latin)—Direction to be silent. Quiet.

♪ Suddenly there was a hush. . . .

⌣ Teneramente (Italian)—Direction to perform delicately and softly, with tenderness.

⌣ "There now, sugar pie, take it easy."

←→ Tenuto (Italian)—Direction to the performer to hold a word for its full value.

←→ "You are one *sly* fox."

♪♪ Tonante (Italian)—To perform in a very loud manner, thundering.

♪♪ "Fi, fi, fo, fum, I smell the blood of an Englishman."

⌘ Tremolo (Italian)—Direction to speak in a trembling, tremulous fashion.

⌘ "Okay, I killed your sister, and brother, and mother, and father. But I still love you."

↑ Velato (Italian)—Direction to perform in a veiled, obscure manner. The opposite of clear and distinct.

↑ "I said, urhhh ghtypt sinnncier."

⤴ Volante (Italian)—Direction to perform lightly and swiftly.

⤴ Suddenly she flew up into the air, higher and higher.

⤴ Zeloso (Italian)—Direction to perform in an energetic, fiery manner.

⤴ "Ha, ha, you sonofagun, I've got you now."

EXERCISES

?"Daryl, how does that song go, 'Bob Dopamino, Mr. Bob Dopamino.'"

"Rock, you're the dopamino. It goes 'Bob Dobolina, Mr. Bob Dobolina.'"

"Okay, okay, so I'm not so good with remembering songs. !But get a load of this, Daryl, up ahead, sashaying down the street like she owned the world, whoooee.

?"Hey, baby, don't I know you from somewhere."

!"Get lost, jerk."

"Let me put it this way, sweetheart. You light my fire."

"Smooth, Rock, smooth."

"Let me say it slowly, and clearly, for you this time. !Get lost, jerk."

"Baby, baby, baby, baby, let me say it for you slowly, like you light my fire."

"Let me say it for you like even more slowly—get lost, jerk."

"Oooooeeee, this time you have done it, I am wounded to the quick."

"She's smiling, Rock."

"Now, baby, my man Daryl here is one of the finest cooks around, and Daryl would like to extend an invite to you to join me and him in an incredible orgy of food, ribs and chicken and stuff, to be held in his backyard this evening at six. ?How does that sound to your ears, baby."

?"Hey, fast-talking smoothie in the very sharp car that needs major repairs, don't you get the message. Get lost, jerk."

?"But baby, you don't want to talk that way to someone whose heart is growing so large it's threatening to jump out of his body any minute, all because of the beautiful woman he sees in front of him, do you."

?"Aren't you Rock, the very same Rock that goes with Pancake. ?Or am I mistaken."

"Let's get out of here, Rock."

"Uh, uh, I could be that Rock, but I'm not saying I am, and I'm not saying I'm not. But tell me, pretty lady. ?How is it that you have heard of that Rock, and how is it that you know about Pancake."

"Because, jerk, I am Pancake's cousin Tallulah, up visiting from Alabama, and I know you wouldn't want me telling Pancake that her best beau Rock tried to pick me up in the street this afternoon and wouldn't let up. ?Am I right, Rock."

"Now that you put it that way, Tallulah, I wouldn't, and I know that a classy lady like yourself would keep that sort of thing to herself, for which I would be mighty appreciative. ?Do you understand me, Tallulah."

"I understand you only too well, Rock. !Now take your friend Daryl, and blow."

"Nice meeting you, Tallulah."

"Yeah, sure."

8

DAZZLE ROCKETS AND BOREDOM BOMBS

🎆 THE DAZZLE ROCKET

There are passages in literature—indeed, in all forms of written work—that are dazzling in their brilliance, in their insight both philosophical and psychological, and that deserve to be pointed out and highlighted for the reader so he may give them proper attention and delight over them. I have in mind the opening of *A Tale of Two Cities*:

> 🎆 It was the best of times, it was the worst of times, it was the age of wisdom, it was the age of foolishness, it was the epoch of belief, it was the epoch of incredulity, it was the season of Light, it was the season of Darkness, it was the spring of hope, it was the winter of despair, we had everything before us, we had nothing before us, we were all going to Heaven, we were all going direct the other way. . . .

I have in mind certain sections of Martin Luther King's "Letter from Birmingham Jail":

> 🎆 Injustice anywhere is a threat to justice everywhere. We are caught in an inescapable network of mutuality, tied in a single garment of destiny. Whatever affects one directly, affects all indirectly.

I have in mind sentences like this one by
C. S. Lewis:

🎆 We struck inland again over the moor
in one of those golden evening lights that
pours a dreamlike mildness over the world.

Or this one from *The Great Gatsby*:

🎆 The wind had blown off, leaving a loud,
bright night with wings beating in the trees
and a persistent organ sound as the full bellows of the earth blew the frogs full of life.

Or this passage from Charles Finney's *Circus
of Dr. Lao*:

🎆 "Well I payed you, read my future."
"Tomorrow will be like today, and day
after tomorrow will be like the day before
yesterday," said Appolonius, "I see your re-
maining days each as a quiet, tedious collec-
tions of hours. You will not travel anywhere.
You will think no new thoughts. You will experience no new passions. Older you will
become but not wiser. Stiffer but not more
dignified. Childless you are, and childless you
shall remain. Of that suppleness you once
commanded in your youth, of that strange
simplicity which once attracted a few men to
you, neither endures, nor shall you recapture
any of them any more. People will talk to you

and visit with you out of sentiment or pity, not because you have anything to offer them. Have you ever seen an old cornstalk turning brown, dying, but refusing to fall over, upon which stray birds alight now and then, hardly remarking what it is they perch on? That is you. I cannot fathom your place in life's economy. A living thing should either create or destroy according to its capacity and caprice, but you, you do neither. You only live on dreaming of the nice things you would like to have happen to you but which never happen; and you wonder vaguely why the young lives about you which you occasionally chide for a fancied impropriety never listen to you and seem to flee at your approach. When you die you will be buried and forgotten and that is all. The morticians will enclose you in a worm-proof casket, thus sealing even unto eternity the clay of your uselessness. And for all the good or evil, creation or destruction, that your living might have accomplished, you might just as well never have lived at all."

❦ THE BOREDOM BOMB

Boredom bombs are just what you thought they were, little bombs to indicate that the "bombed" prose you are about to read, or have just read, is tired and tedious, that it probably contains tryptophan or some other noxious amino acid that will put you to sleep any moment now. "Aha," you may say, "if I read it, I'll know whether or not it is boring. I don't need you or anyone else to tell me."

True and not true. If you haven't read the particular boring passage or tome yet, then you might appreciate someone warning you, just as you might appreciate a review of a film or book just coming out. No one can read or see everything. No one has the time. We must be discriminating; we must make choices about what we read. And if you are forewarned but must read the text anyway because it is important, or relevant, or of abiding interest to you, then go ahead, but perhaps you will read faster or slower because of a dazzle rocket or boredom bomb.

But what if you have already read the text? Certainly there can be no possible reason to have someone point out that it is boring. Maybe so, but wouldn't it be important if you agreed with the assessment? Then the next time you saw a boredom bomb you might approach the bombed text differently. Cumulatively this could make your reading more efficient, save you wasted time.

So when does the author or the editor indicate something is boring? They indicate it when they know something is boring but they must include it for purposes of scholarly completeness, or reaffirmation, or example, or tribute, or obligation of one kind or another. Perhaps Melville or his publisher could have indicated that the chapters on cetology in *Moby Dick* might not be of interest to persons uninterested in such matters, that the novel could still be understood if you skipped those chapters, that the reader was heading into deep waters or muddy shoals. Of course if you are a cetologist or have an abiding interest in such studies, these chapters could prove endlessly fascinating. You will have to make that decision for yourself. Thus we have empty or unshaded boredom bombs to indicate that not everyone will find the marked passage boring—there are exceptions and some may find it interesting or exciting. But they are exceptions. Have you noticed a boredom bomb attached to this exposition? What can I say?

Dazzle rockets and boredom bombs are not objective and definitive. They are subjective and meant only as a guide for the reader. When you see them, you must understand them as such and proceed according to instinct. They are the grammatical analog of signs along a road you must traverse that say FALLING ROCKS AHEAD or ROAD BEING REPAIRED. You must take the road but you are forewarned that conditions are less than favorable or could be troublesome. If the road is sufficiently awful, you may take another road.

The following are classically ho hum despite the fact that they are penned by otherwise talented or even great writers. This from Thackeray's *The Rose and the King*:

🔻 And then the monarch went on to argue in his own mind (though we need not say that blank verse is not argument) that what he had got it was his duty to keep, and that, if at one time he had entertained ideas of a certain

restitution, which shall be nameless, the pros-
pect by a certain marriage of uniting two
crowns and two nations which had been en-
gaged in bloody and expensive wars, as the
Paflagonians and the Crimeans had been, put
the idea of Giglio's restoration to the throne
out of the question: nay, were his own brother,
King Savio, alive, he would certainly will
away the crown from his own son in order to
bring about such a desirable union.

Or this from *The Mensa Think Smart Book*, by
Salny and Frumkes:

⬇ Now make up a sentence in which each
numeral is represented by a word with the
same number of letters. If the number is 143,
you could memorize "I work yet." If it hap-
pened to be the address of Joe Jones, you
might make up a sentence like "I know Joe."
This would have the double advantage of re-
minding you that it is Joe's number, and of
fixing the number firmly in your mind in
association with Joe. Try it for the three sets
of numbers you have listed above.

Need I explain, it's good old Form 1040:

⬇ Subtract the amount on line 9g, if any,
from the amount on line 8a. . . .
If line 10 is zero, stop here and attach
this form to your return.

If you answered "Yes" on line 2, go to line 11 now.

If you are reporting this sale on the installment method, stop here and see line 1b instructions.

All others, stop here and enter the amount from line 10 on Schedule D, line 3 or line 10.

And how about some words on irreversibility from the *Encyclopedia of Physics*:

⬇ Physical systems commonly display a tendency to change spontaneously from one state to another, but not to change in the opposite direction. Examples are the tendency of heat to pass from regions of high temperature to regions of low temperature, the tendency of mechanical or electrical energy to be transformed into heat by friction of resistance, and the mixing or diffusion of different substances. While irreversibility appears to be an obvious feature of macroscopic natural phenomena, so much so that violations of this tendency are scarcely conceivable, it is not yet established whether it should be considered a general law applicable on both the atomic and the cosmological scales. Most physicists accept the "statistical" explanation of irreversibility, according to which complex systems with many degrees of freedom tend to spread out among more and more diverse states in the "phase space" of possible configurations. (See Statistical Mechanics.)

Even physicists soon doze off unless they are statistical mechanics who are on a roll.

Or consider these immortal thoughts from Robert of *Robert's Rules of Order*:

⬇ The effect of an amendment may be obtained by calling for, or moving, the previous question or a different set of the pending questions (which must be consecutive and include the immediately pending question), in which case the vote is taken first on the motion which orders the previous question on the largest number of questions.

SYMBOL SUMMARY

DAZZLE ROCKETS AND BOREDOM BOMBS

🎆 THE DAZZLE ROCKET—Indicates literary brilliance.

⬇ THE BOREDOM BOMB—Indicates tiresome prose that will put you to sleep.

EXERCISES

EXERCISE A

In my house we all seem to want a different dog. My daughter Amber likes long, sausage-type dogs, dachshunds and basset hounds. Son Tim likes hunting dogs, Labs and retrievers. My wife fancies poodles. Personally, I like boxers or Rhodesian Ridgebacks, something big and strong that pulls and tugs, that lets you know it's there on the other end of the leash. Not one of those high-strung, shivering toy breeds that make you feel as though you're walking a squirrel. They just quiver and shake. The vibrating drives you crazy. In fact, when they are frightened they shake so fast they become blurry. What fun is a dog you can't see clearly?

Which reminds me of Weimaraners and Dobermans. These dogs resemble Stealth airplanes. They are colored in such a way that you almost don't see them coming, especially at night. And they move quickly and quietly. Before you know it the Doberman is by your side looking up at your throat as if it's a bacon cheeseburger with grilled onions. Where did he come from? Go 'way, doggie. Weimaraners, for their part, slip around you and into the park without your even seeing them. Known as gray ghosts, they take the gray ghost thing very seriously.

And what about the king of dogs, the giant Great Dane? This majestic animal is your size, and by nature has big, long, low-flapping ears, very much like your grandfather. Luckily your grandfather is toilet-trained, unlike the Great Dane. Ever try to mop up Lake Erie? Danes do everything in a big way.

My daughter Amber loves any dog as long as it is a puppy. Puppies are *sooo* cute. Amber doesn't realize that in a few blinks, the Dane puppy grows up into a big, loud, frisky adult dog, the size of a horse, that jumps on your chest and licks your nose when you least expect it, like now. "Down, Blitzen, down, boy!"

Amber also likes any dog that waddles, or has sad eyes. Thus, cocker spaniels, basset hounds and misformed beagles often catch her eye.

"He's *sooo* cute, Dad. Let's get him."

"But that's a pit bull, Amber—he's trained to do war tricks like finishing off a battalion."

"Look, Dad, he's smiling at us."

"Sharks look like they're smiling too, Amber."

"No, Dad, Butcho wants us to take him home."

Curiously, Butcho's teeth are six times the size of his body; our canine adviser informs us he uses them as a tool to open cans of food. Butcho is better equipped, I think, to chew tanks or go after hardened criminals. Butcho's role model/mentor at the kennel was a crocodile.

When selecting a dog, consider also that your dog will tend to attract other leashed dogs and their masters when you walk him. So if you want to be alone, choose a wolf. People will avoid you. But if you wish to invite the opposite sex, because you are single, let us say, or adventurous, choose a gregarious dog of some indistinguishable breed. A mutt. This will force the other owner to inquire as to what kind of dog you have. The rest is up to you.

Also, remember how dogs look like their masters. Thus, athletic types own sporting dogs; beautiful women, Afghans; and princes, Borzois. If you are a wimp, try to choose a dog that will change your image, not encourage it, and stay away from Chihuahuas and Pomeranians. Even a six-foot-seven, 260-pound nose tackle for the Steelers looks ridiculous walking a Pomeranian named Killer.

If you're having a hard time making up your mind, or if the members of your family can't agree, maybe you'll discover that the dog of your dreams is just that. After all, the dog of your dreams won't leave any signature on the carpets of your reality.
—*Lewis Burke Frumkes*

EXERCISE B

"You know, Rock, I hate boring people."

"Me too, Daryl. It's good that we're not boring."

"I'm certainly not boring, Rock. I always include facts in my conversation. ?For example, did you know that George Washington invented the electric typewriter."

?"Is that a fact, Daryl."

?"Would I make something like that up, Rock."

"Naw, of course you wouldn't, Daryl."

"I'm also really into weather, Rock."

?"What do you mean by that, Daryl."

"I love weather reports. They turn me on."

?"Weather reports turn you on, Daryl."

"Yeah. I especially love foul weather. Rain, storms, clouds, low temperatures."

"You're very strange, Daryl."

"Not really, Rock. Everybody has a hobby. Mine is weather."

"That's great, Daryl, but I wouldn't tell too many people about it, if you know what I mean."

?"What's your hobby, Rock."

"My hobby is an interesting one, Daryl. I collect old motorcycle boots. Now that's an interesting hobby."

?"Motorcycle boots. ?Who's interested in motorcycle boots."

?"I am, Daryl. ?Who's interested in weather."

"Let's get out of here, Rock."

!"Shit. It's raining again."

9

LITERAL AND FIGURATIVE PUNCTUATION

LITERAL PUNCTUATION

Sometimes it is very difficult to distinguish between literal and figurative language. When that special someone says to you, "Go jump in the lake," does she mean it literally or figuratively? Sometimes you can tell from an easy context. On a hot summer's day, for example, when you are sweltering after a basketball game, it might be just the thing to cool you off.

On that same hot summer's day, however, when there is no basketball game, and you have offended her in some way like with your twelve jokes about the time she fell in her soup, it might just mean she is cooling off on you. And I don't blame her a bit; you are gross beyond belief.

Other times you may not be able to tell so easily. So before you respond hotly and wrongly to her urging you to "Go jump in the lake" or anything else, try looking for the veritas sign, which will indicate whether or not you are literally to go jump in the lake. The lake, by the way, is down the hill to your left. You will recognize it when you see it . . . large and wet, clear and rippled.

☺   **THE VERITAS SIGN**

Veritas means "truth" in Latin—not that we are speaking Latin, so what else is new. We have conscripted *veritas* here to mean "literal truth"—that what you are reading is to be taken literally or truly.

Thus, ☺ "She screamed like a banshee" means literally that she screamed like a banshee—actually something like this: "Aieeeeeeeeeeeeee-ooooooo!" "She screamed like a banshee" without a veritas sign, however, means she went "yoooow-hoooo." Sort of like an owl rather than a banshee. Get the difference?

Let's try another:

☺ He stuck to her like glue.

With the veritas sign this sentence means he literally stuck to her and couldn't be removed without ripping him off her dress. Whereas without the veritas sign, "He stuck to her like glue" means he followed her and wouldn't let her out of his sight. Perhaps he thought she was a spy and he was McGonagle of the FBI.

Let's try one more:

☺ "You are a fool, Jack."

With a veritas sign this sentence means that Jack is actually a fool by trade, or joker. He is the kind of fool you see attending the king, wearing a fool's cap and a multicolored waistcoat, and carrying a scepter, and whose job it is to divert or entertain the king. When the king summons Jack, Jack appears, full of corny jokes and witty advice.

Of course, if there is no veritas sign in evidence, then the sentence probably means that Jack is a fool in the sense of being foolish, or not smart, rather than a fool by trade. This Jack is just your ordinary husband, probably a stockbroker or accountant. Is he really a fool? Don't ask his wife.

In the latter instance, though, shouldn't there be a punctuation mark to indicate the sentence is a figure of speech and not to be taken literally? Or is the absence of a veritas sign enough?

Well, it just happens there is a sign to indicate figures of speech more clearly than just the absence of the veritas sign, and that sign is:

< **THE NOT**

The not sign indicates, for example, that Jack is not literally a fool, but a fool in the metaphorical sense. Thus Jack does not occupy a place in the king's court, much as he might like to; rather he suffers indignities about his foolhardiness at the hands of his family and friends.

< !"Go blow it out your ear, Franz."

Uh-oh, there is a not sign in this sentence. Thus we know that Franz is being told off only in a figurative sense, not being told to blow something out of his ear as if he were spouting like Jonah's whale.

＜ "I'm going to explode any moment."

Again, there is a not sign present; thus we don't have to leave the area for fear that Fred is going to literally burst in all directions at once like a giant nova—not Nova Scotia salmon,＜ you fool (again note the not with fool), but a nova as in galaxy, star suddenly growing brighter, etc. Fred will not burst; he is merely angry and feels as if he is going to burst. Poor Fred!

Do you remember when you were a kid and it was all the rage to describe a girl with funny figures of speech?

＜ "Her cheeks are like peaches—round, yellow, and fuzzy."

＜ "Her teeth are like stars—they come out at night."

＜ "Her hair is like a small town—sparsely populated."

But for the not sign, someone might have taken you seriously.

⊖ THE EXAGGERATION MARK

The exaggeration mark figures (excuse the pun) here too. For exaggeration is a kind of figure. If we say, for example, she grew like a weed, we are exaggerating her rate of growth, but it is not quite a figure. In any event I'll include it in this chapter.

How do we know that when Marnie says that something is the size of a bread box, or a house, or a planet, she is exaggerating? Maybe it really is.

Answer: We know she is exaggerating because there is an exaggeration mark present. Otherwise we would have to take Marnie literally and there would be a veritas sign.

So we see that exaggeration is a kind of figure, but a special kind of figure. Now the question is, do we use one exaggeration mark no matter the size of the exaggeration? Actually there is an informal rule that applies.

With the bread box, one exaggeration mark is sufficient. With the house, two exaggeration marks should be used. And with the planet, three exaggeration marks are probably necessary. Thus the rule with exaggeration marks is to use them in multiples according to the order of the exaggeration. The larger the exaggeration away from the truth, the more exaggeration marks must be used.

⊖⊖⊖After winning the lotto sweepstakes, his head swelled so, it began to lift his body off the ground until he floated off into the clouds.

This remark deserves at least three exaggeration marks. Although now that I look at his head, maybe two exaggeration marks would have been enough. Wow! That's some sized head. Shoot him down, somebody!

And now we segue into another variation on the exaggeration.

☙"I'm afraid, Lewis, I could beat Anatoly Karpov if he was playing your position."

"Is that right, Richard? . . . Checkmate."

Richard has exaggerated the strength of his chess position, or his own playing ability, without being aware of it. What do we do in such a situation?

Is he boasting, or trying to intimidate his opponent?

Both are forms of exaggeration. Thus we must use the boast sign, when appropriate, or the intimidation mark.

---

6   THE BOAST

The boast is used much like the exaggeration mark. A small boast such as:

6"I can beat you in checkers."

deserves one boast.

However:

66"I am the world's greatest lover."

deserves two or three boasts. Sorry, Pancake's testimony doesn't change anything.

And if a man writes a book with chapters entitled:

6 Why I am so wise

6 Why I am so clever

6 Why I write such good books

6 Why I am a destiny

is he boasting, is he calling it as he sees it, or is he merely having a little fun at our expense? These titles, it so happens, are the chapter headings of *Ecce Homo*, Friedrich Nietzsche's strange autobiographical work written in 1888 just before he went mad. Make of them what you will, and assign boasts also if you will.

6   THE INTIMIDATION MARK

Sometimes a boast functions more as a means to intimidate an opponent than as an actual belief in the speaker's prowess. Thus a boxer will often boast about what he will do to his opponent once the fight starts, hoping to win the fight before he even enters the ring. When this is the case, we add an arrow to the end of the boast and make it an intimidation mark.

♂ "I will teach that Goliath of Gath—an ugly bear if ever I saw one—a lesson he will not soon forget. You can bet your silver and gold on it. One shot from my sling, and wham. Down goes Goliath for the count."

And sometimes it works. The opponent becomes so psyched out and intimidated that he loses the fight psychologically before he even comes to blows. In this case an intimidation mark is definitely in order.

♂?"Think you can play that passage, eh. Bach himself couldn't make it halfway through."

Intimidation, intimidation.
Even a literary passage can be intimidating:

♂ It is a tale told by an idiot, full of sound and fury, signifying nothing. (Shakespeare, *Macbeth*)

The converse of intimidate is to be intimidated, and there is an entire constellation of signs to indicate when someone is shy, demure, intimidated, submissive, or otherwise cowed. Not everyone is a dominant, intimidating type, you know.

For those less-than-arrogant, anti-aggressive souls, we have the following signs:

•¦• THE MEEK SIGN—Indicates that the individual is of a more sensitive nature, that he or she is responding submissively.

•¦•"Okay, if you say so."

•¦•?"Do you think it would be all right if I went to the bathroom."

•¦•"No, of course, I would never do anything like that."

The double meek, of course, indicates extreme submissiveness.

•¦• •¦•?"Would you like to use me as a doormat and step all over my face."

ρ THE SORRY—Yet another variation on the meek, intimidated, submissive theme. Sorry people are sorry about everything, even that they are being sorry. The sorry should be used when one is feeling remorse or regret or just intimidation.

ρ"I didn't mean to say that."

ρ"Sorry, sorry."

ρ"Please forgive me, please, please."

If the person is extremely sorry or very, very sorry, more than one sorry should be used.

But how do we show that someone is not necessarily intimidated or sorry or submissive, but rather he is just reticent by nature, demure, shy?

⧫ THE SHY—Indicates shyness, reticence. The larger the shy, the more reticent the individual. It is an inverse proportion sign.

⧫ "I'm happy to make your acquaintance."

⧫ "My name is Marguerita. . . ."

⧫ "Please don't watch me while I do this."

Beyond shyness and intimidation, there are signs to indicate patronage, disinterest, aloofness, coolness.

✓ THE CONDESCENSION SIGN—Shows that one person is looking down upon another—is patronizing the other. It is a form of snobbery that occurs, unfortunately, all too often.

✓ "That's very good, Rock. Now see if you can add three and three."

✓? "Did you hear. Patrick was just promoted to assistant sweep in housekeeping."

✔"That's a lovely hat, dear. Maybe I can use it for my cat in the Easter parade."

◠ THE COOL—Indicates like hip, man. Someone who is cool has true sophistication, mingles easily and comfortably with all types, displays grace under pressure, and does not react foolishly to provocation. Marlon Brando is cool, Henry Kissinger is cool, Clint Eastwood is cool, Grace Kelly is cool, Jack Nicholson is cool.

However, used alone, the cool sign can also indicate disinterest or aloofness.

◠?"Were you speaking to me."

◠"Uh-huh . . . uh-huh."

◣ THE ULTRACOOL—If there is any doubt about whether a person is cool or just disinterested or aloof, use the ultracool.

◣"That's a mighty big piece you've got pointing at me, my friend."

◣"I'd like to redeem this lotto ticket for the fifty million, please."

◣"Simmer down, there, big boy, we all make mistakes."

SYMBOL SUMMARY

LITERAL AND FIGURATIVE PUNCTUATION

☺ **THE VERITAS SIGN**—Indicates something is meant literally.

< **THE NOT**—Indicates something or someone is not literal but metaphorical.

⊖ **THE EXAGGERATION MARK**—Clear indication that something is being exaggerated.

6 **THE BOAST**—Similar to exaggeration, but used for purposes of self-inflation.

6 **THE INTIMIDATION MARK**—A boast which is used to intimidate.

•¦• **THE MEEK SIGN**—Indicates degree of submissiveness, sensitivity.

ρ **THE SORRY**—Indicates remorse, regret, intimidation.

〞 **THE SHY**—Used to indicate reticence or shyness.

√• **THE CONDESCENSION SIGN**—Used to indicate patronage, or one person looking down upon another.

◁ **THE COOL**—The cool may indicate true sophistication, acts of grace under pressure, a natural ability to deal with difficult situations, or maybe just aloofness or disinterest.

● THE ULTRACOOL—When in doubt as to whether a single cool indicates true coolness or just aloofness or disinterest, use the ultracool.

EXERCISES

"Hey, Rock. ?How about let's go mountain climbing."

?"Mountain climbing. ?Daryl, do I look like a human fly. Just because I climbed into Jenny the Crab's window the other night, and she lives on the fourth floor, doesn't mean I want to go mountain climbing. ?Understand, Daryl."

"Oh, c'mon, Rock. Everybody has to climb a mountain sometime in his life. I thought today would be a good day."

"Daryl, I think you do not have all your laces tied, or something. I told you even though I could be one of the great mountain climbers, I do not have any interest. ?Do you get my point."

"But Rock, you'll love it. I've got some old ropes and spikes down in my basement."

"Daryl, let me make it clear. If we went mountain climbing, I would probably be coming down the mountain while you were still climbing up. ?Now I would not want to do that to you, Daryl, do you understand."

"Hey, Rock. ?How about we call the girls and go to the movies."

?"What's playing, Daryl."

"*North by Northwest*."

?"*North by Northwest*. ?The one with Cary Grant. Daryl, Daryl, you are something else."

10

TRANSITIONAL METAPUNCTUATION

It is not easy to make transitions from one text to another, or even from one subject to another. How, for example, do you get from collard greens to problems in topology, or from the teleological argument for the existence of God to aerobic typing? The answer, of course, is transitions. However, transitions can often seem factitious because the writer does not really have a transition in mind—he simply wants to get from text A to text B in the easiest way possible. In the interests of style and rhetoric, he is frequently forced to contrive transitions. This is wasteful of effort and often obvious. Wouldn't it be in everyone's best interest if the author could insert a transition mark of some kind when appropriate and just get to where he wants to go without doing a little literary dance?

To this end, I have created several metatransitions such as the paralingual to mark transitions between similar or parallel subjects, the crosstextual to join texts falling within normal subject ranges, and the hypercross to mark transitions between writings of highly disparate or opposing content. There are also marks to indicate time shifting, place shifting, and viewpoint shifting, which we will touch on as well. For those of you interested in shapeshifting, you're reading the wrong book. Sorry.

♫ THE PARALINGUAL

The paralingual is an extremely useful little device when you have finished talking about one thing and want to get to the next related thing without pausing and losing your train of thought.

I have capitalized the next thoughts here just to make this clear—this is usually not necessary.

"Tell me about Vegas, Rock."

♫"Well, Daryl and I were about to break the bank in Vegas WHEN IN WALKS SALLY MCGREGOR."

?"Were you in love with Sally McGregor, Rock."

♫"Sally McGregor is some piece of work. LET ME TELL YOU, WHEN SHE AND I WERE FIFTEEN . . ."

♫"We were on this expedition, and there was a cave. SO . . . in she went and there was the giant spider. Now, I don't know how you feel about spiders, but . . ."

?"Do you feel all right, Rock."

♫?"AS I WAS SAYING . . . directed panspermia is one of the likelier ways in which life came to this planet, *n'est-ce pas.*"

"Rock, I didn't know you were so well read."

Without the paralingual, the writer would be accused of writing choppy, unpleasant prose.

even though the reader probably wants to hear about Sally McGregor as much as the writer wants to write about her. When these motives dovetail, the paralingual is important to move the prose along.

≠ THE CROSSTEXTUAL

The crosstextual takes the reader smoothly from one subject to the other without the reader having to ponder or figure out if there was a transition. The crosstextual tells you there was. Unlike the paralingual, it is almost invisible.

≠ OF COURSE NOT ALL RADICALS ARE FREE RADICALS. Unlike unpaired electrons, political radicals have little freedom at all. They are slaves to their philosophy, to their ideology.

≠ "LET ME TELL YOU ABOUT THE TIME JEB AND I went down to the cave and played roller derby with the bats."

≠ ANOTHER FORM OF DOUBLE TALK IS the kind where you don't even realize the writer is talking about writers talking.

THE HYPERCROSS

The hypercross joins ideas of very different tempers that on the surface may seem incompatible or even diametrically opposed. It is like the ultimate peacemaker, taking Arabs and Israelis, and allowing them to be heard in the same forum.

#"BELIEVE IT OR NOT . . . black is my favorite color."
"I love white . . . it goes with everything."

#"REMARKABLY . . . on the surface he seems charitable and free of the usual manipulative tricks."
"Allow me to introduce you. Rock, this is Nicolo Machiavelli."

#"TRUTH TO TELL . . . I hate her."
"I love her."

#?"I KNOW THIS SEEMS RIDICULOUS, BUT . . . much as we are talking about nutrition and health, is there a synthetic a priori."

← **TIME TRANSITIONS**

Time transitions keep readers moving along a chronological path toward events that are strung out like pearls on a necklace. Sometimes the transitions move forward, and sometimes they move back. Sometimes they even flash back. Generally they are marked by an arrow to signal direction in time, followed by a number to denote year, month, minute, or whatever unit of time is being discussed.

←12 "YEARS AGO, when I was just starting out as a con man . . ."

1→ "We will all begin to grow bananas in the garden next year."

In the case of seasons, the arrow is followed by one, two, three, or four, to show which season. Spring is considered the first season.

3→ "ROCK AND DARYL set out for Xanadu."

When a holiday such as Christmas is involved, an icon such as a wreath or stocking is appropriate.

✿ We all returned to Chicago to commemorate when we first met in Lonny's bar.

---

o→ **PLACE SHIFTING**

Place or location transitions are ways of telling the reader that he is now somewhere else, of moving him across great distances at the speed of light.

←o MEANWHILE BACK IN PALM BEACH, the Billion-Dollar Ball was just getting under way.

o→ ON THE OTHER SIDE OF THE ATLANTIC, IN DRESDEN, Maria was pining away.

♂ VIEWPOINT SHIFTING

Viewpoints shift from one side of an issue to the other, sometimes subtly, other times with little warning.

♂?"GRANTED, but have you considered that women are humans too."

♂!"AHA. Now I've got you. . . ."

♂INDEED, it is said that beanies with propellers are a thing of the past.

SYMBOL SUMMARY

TRANSITIONAL METAPUNCTUATION

⚡ THE PARALINGUAL—Makes the transition from one thing to another without pausing.

≠ THE CROSSTEXTUAL—Is a smooth, almost invisible transition from one subject to another.

THE HYPERCROSS—Joins ideas that might on the surface seem opposite or incompatible.

← TIME TRANSITIONS—Indicate movement forward or backward in time.

o→ PLACE SHIFTING—Indicates place transitions.

⚥ VIEWPOINT SHIFTING—Indicates viewpoint transitions.

EXERCISES

The problem is not, as most people think, how to make contact with just any life forms from outer space; the problem is how to make contact with affluent life forms from outer space. We need space intelligences who not only understand our language and customs, but can infuse our economy with new capital and ideas.

"X1-2 to Chemical Bank. X1-2 to Chemical Bank. Message received. I am teleporting thirty-five billion dollars in fresh cash to your main office. Do you read? I am teleporting thirty-five billion dollars in fresh cash to your main office."

Who needs to wake up to some creatures from the Crab Galaxy who are poor as church mice and want to suck our blood because they don't have any of their own? These horrible characters will come down, as all the movies have shown, disguised as your best friend, maybe Rock or Daryl, and then, zowie, when you're not looking, bite you in the neck and turn you into one of them. More drag on the society. Stay out of that Crab Galaxy, will you? They're no good up there.

Thank God, the president of Chemical Bank knows X1-2. A buddy is a buddy. And there is more cash where X1-2 comes from. I haven't told you about X1-3 or X1-4. Talk about affluent. Whooooie! These guys buy planets just for the fun of it. One of them is even a limited partner in Kohlberg, Kravis. Big bucks. X1-4, for example, keeps a place on Ganymede in our own solar system just for those few times when he's transacting a deal here. His home on Sirius B, a white dwarf, just 8.7 light-years away, is absolutely incredible. It's about 25 acres of rolling Sirian landscape, fantastic views, and unequaled sunsets. Of course, Sirius B is not everybody's ideal vacation spot. It has a tropical climate and an 8,000-degree surface temperature, so you have to like hot weather. Its atmospheric density is a million times that of earth, so the inhabitants there tend to be rather two-dimensional. But they are rich, those Sirians. Besides, they can slip through keyholes and under the door.

The point is, earth needs affluent friends like the Sirians from outer space, especially when everyone is announcing a new endowment campaign. There are limits, as we have seen, to both our natural resources and our capital supply. Can you imagine if there were another energy crisis? It could spell real trouble. But with contacts and help from other worlds, we could survive. We could mine some of the abundant interstellar gas clouds that are just drifting around the universe.

Let me illustrate another possible solution to such a crisis. Venusians have often been described by astronomers as floating gas bags, which they resent because it has funny connotations. But the truth is they are loaded with gas and more than willing to part with some if properly approached. The proper approach, incidentally, is not, "Geez, does he stink!" It is important that when making contact with affluent life forms from other worlds, we do not insult them just because they are different from us. We must be diplomatic.

Only recently a hip radio telescopist on Arecibo made contact with some affluent life forms on Alpha Centauri and, assuming they were friendly, requested a loan.

"Hey, man, you got twenty dollars?"

The Alpha Centaurians zapped him with a particle beam. Alpha Centaurians are neither friendly nor particularly generous. Lesson: Never press an alien for money unless you know him well. Alpha Centaurians are like pit bulls when it comes to a buck.

Nevertheless, establishing contact with affluent life from outer space is what this country needs to get us out of the rut we're in. We are going around in economic circles, or cycles if you prefer. Inflation, deflation, recession, depression, inflation, deflation, recession, depression. Sometimes we go right from inflation to depression. No other planet operates in this manner. It's no good. For years, aliens have been nibbling at our securities anyway and making money, just like the Japanese. Boesky was an affluent alien. There is a star in the constellation "Arb" full of Boeskies. Where do you think he got all that inside information? Most of it he took from other people's heads, directly. Unfortunately for him he also started taking information from some unsavory characters within the financial community. He really didn't need it. He was just trying so hard to be like an earthling. I suspect Carl Icahn is also an alien though I can't prove it. If I'm correct, TWA will probably begin introducing flying saucers into their regular fleet within the next ten years. That will be a sure sign.

The Russians, too, are trying to make contact with affluent creatures from outer space. Yeltsin is no fool. He wants to discourage star wars and curry star cash. Star cash is one hundred percent fungible and is used as a standard throughout the universe. Other affluent civilizations are full of it.

From this man's point of view, if America is to survive into the twenty-first century, it is time we established both contact with affluent life in outer space and credit.

11

FUTURE AND EXPERIMENTAL PUNCTUATION

As technology marches forward and language becomes ever more complex and rich, new punctuation systems, beyond even metapunctuation, will appear. Future punctuation may include using colors for punctuating or notating, which for the moment seems impractical because of printing costs. At such time that color becomes feasible, we might read red for anger, for example (perhaps light anger would be pink, hot anger, deep crimson).

Or words may appear three-dimensionally, accompanied by sound so that light verse would look and sound like raindrops, while "Fee fie fo fum" might resemble giant blocks of granite and sound like thunder.

With the development of multimedia computers and new software, self-punctuating programs will become as common as spell-check programs are today. Headsets that monitor the author's ideas and inflections will communicate interactively with the punctuation program to get the meanings right.

In time, other new language technologies will emerge—photoelectric, laser, chemical, biological, electronic, and telepathic.

Communication with other life forms in other galaxies as well as on the bacterial and microscopic levels will eventually take place.

The need for effective communication will become ever more important as the language grows and proliferates, so long as there are beings to communicate.

But what about metapunctuation and statements about the future? Well, we do have possibility marks, perhaps signs, and tentativos. These are used to indicate different degrees of potentiality. For example:

♩ THE POSSIBILITY MARK

Suppose the sense of a meeting is that something is possible. The reader needs to know this. Thus a possibility mark creates a mood of hopefulness, where heretofore only darkness reigned.

♩ "In the future, scientists may develop new punctuation that is commensurate with future communication needs. At least we would like to believe so."

Here, the possibility mark reinforces the probability that new punctuation will be developed. We are splitting hairs here, but if there is doubt, the possibility mark emphasizes the positive mood.

On the other hand, the tentativo is less positive.

TT   THE TENTATIVO

TT "We'll get back to you soon."

In this instance, "We'll get back to you soon" could be positive or negative. The inflection is not clear. A tentativo at the start of a sentence suggests that the powers that be were not positively disposed to the interviewee, for example, and probably will render a negative judgment.

⅒   THE PERHAPS SIGN

A perhaps sign, on the other hand, means the judgment can go either way. Perhaps is on the fence. Things could turn out positively or negatively. When there is no valence for good or for bad, a perhaps sign is the way to go.

⅒?"Helloooo-oh, anybody out there."

SYMBOL SUMMARY

FUTURE PUNCTUATION

⚲ THE POSSIBILITY MARK—Indicates that something is possible, hopeful.

TT THE TENTATIVO—Suggests that something is tentative, hanging by a thread.

⚏ THE PERHAPS SIGN—Indicates that a judgment can go either way.

EXERCISES

?"So, Rock, do you have a date with Jenny the Crab tonight or not."

"Easy, Daryl. If I had a date with Jenny the Crab, I wouldn't tell you, because you might go back and tell Pancake. ?Isn't that so, Daryl."

"Never, Rock. I'm your friend. ?Would I mess you up with Pancake by telling her about Jenny the Crab."

?"Can I trust you, Daryl. ?Can you keep a secret."

"Of course, Rock. I'm a clam."

"Jenny said she's waiting for me."

?"Does that mean you're going to see her or not."

"It means I can see her if I want, Daryl. ?*Capice*."

"*No capice*, Rock. I do not understand what you are talking about. Either you have a date with Jenny the Crab or you do not have a date with Jenny the Crab. ?Which is it, Rock."

"You are correct, Daryl. I may have a date with Jenny, but I can't tell you. ?Does that make sense, Daryl."

"Sort of, Rock. It means that maybe you don't trust me. ?Is that it."

"Sort of, Daryl. It's not really that I don't trust you, it's that I'm afraid of Pancake. ?Now do you understand."

"Yeah, I understand, Rock. So now I can't tell you if I have a date with Lizzie the Lizard tonight."

"I hope you do, Daryl."

"Me too, Rock. See you around."

"Yeah, Daryl. See you around."

●